1000 Words

1000 Words
Writer Conversations

Introduction
Lucy Soutter

(Sites of Struggle: Surveying the Relationship between Writing and Photography)

*Lucy Soutter is an artist, critic and art historian.
She is Course Leader of MA Photography Arts at the
University of Westminster, and is the author of* Why Art
Photography? *(Routledge, 2nd ed. 2018), translated into
Spanish, Chinese, Korean and Farsi. A founding partner
of the Global Photographies Network, her current research
explores expanded photographic practices, contemporary
narrative and issues of cultural translation.*

The relation of photography and language is a principal site of struggle for value and power in contemporary representations of reality; it is the place where images and words find and lose their conscience, their aesthetic and ethical identity.
— W. J. T. Mitchell, *Picture Theory* (Chicago: University of Chicago Press, 1995, p. 281)

This collection offers unique insights into the work of contemporary photography writers. Chosen to offer a balance of established and emerging voices and a range of international perspectives, the 16 writers work in different genres and from within various disciplines – in several cases, across more than one. Many are academics whose understanding is shaped by research and teaching. Several are creative practitioners with a built-in awareness of the impulses for making. Most contribute to the lively criticism that takes place across current magazines, journals and online platforms. Each has been chosen for their timely, distinctive approach. Together, our dialogues with them map a vibrant field of activity.

Why is photography writing important at this moment in history? Of course, anyone can look at photographs without reading anything, but to do so will always throw us back on our own assumptions, whatever context we carry in our own minds. Words – inside, outside and alongside the image – generate additional layers of meaning. The relationship between writing and photography is not always harmonious. Words are frequently used to shape the context and thrust of an image, in the process risking overreach. In the power relationship between the two, words exert a stronger force for exposition, yet photographs have a visceral force that can never be fully contained by language. The inexhaustible visuality of the photographic image can open onto almost every academic discipline, every field of human endeavour. It is no wonder that the history of writing about photography has been so rich. Although sometimes labelled an obsolete medium, photography and its discourses continue to lie at the centre of contemporary culture, shaping the way we represent and understand the world. Photography writers are as crucial as photographers to this important work.

Since its appearance, the photograph has been twinned, dogged and haunted by writing. Novelists, poets, humourists, political commentators and art critics all put pen to paper to address

    Lucy Soutter

photography in the 19th century. Then, as now, a medium so closely tied to our perception of the world provided writers with a richly generative source of comment and criticism which they could link back to their own key concerns. A highly descriptive writer like Edgar Allen Poe could marvel at the uncanny precision of the daguerreotype process. A poet of the imagination like Charles Baudelaire could express contempt at the camera's slavish fidelity to banal appearances. A critic of art and literature like Lady Elizabeth Eastlake could decry the aesthetic 'deficiencies' of photographic art, at the same time as identifying the staggering potential of photomechanical reproduction more broadly.

Writing has taken many creative forms alongside photography, from the surrealism of André Breton's photo-illustrated novel *Nadja* (1928) to the brutal photo-epigrams of Bertolt Brecht's *War Primer* (1955), and from the tender fictive documentary of Langston Hughes and Roy de Carava's *The Sweet Flypaper of Life* (1955) to the evocative mysteries of W.G. Sebald's photographically-punctuated novel *Austerlitz* (2001). Artist-photographers have been amongst those using images to activate the space of creative writing, in turn catalysing new possibilities for photography. Teju Cole and Moyra Davey are two striking recent examples.

In the mid-20th century, academic writing about photography was primarily art historical with scholars and curators such as Lucia Moholy, Helmut and Alison Gernsheim and Beaumont Newhall undertaking some of the first historical surveys. Alongside the work of selection, description, classification and interpretation, early historians of photography were necessarily occupied with validation. They worked towards a set of shared values for an omnipresent medium which struggled to be taken seriously until its emergence in the art market in the 1980s. Whilst photography spread across the globe within years of its invention, photography writing outside of Western centres of activity took place mostly in newspapers and magazines rather than academic texts. One of the key tasks for photography scholars in the 21st century has been to broaden the historical map for photography, recover period images and, in turn, recuperate the writings that may have been produced alongside them. As explored in the volume *Curator Conversations*, curators also play a key part in this ongoing activity, both through their writing and exhibitions.

The history of photographic criticism offers another rich thread in photography writing, from the aesthetic, literary reviews accompanying the Pictorialist salons of the 1890s to the social engagement of the New York Photo League's *Photo Notes* in the 1930s and 40s, and from the expressive subjectivity of Minor White's early 1950s *Aperture* reviews to the activist bent of UK publications like *Ten.8* and *Camerawork* in the 1970s and 80s. Allowing writers to bring their own agendas to the table along with the issues of the day, criticism continues to offer a bridge between the most advanced insider debates around the different branches of photography and the diverse audiences who follow them. The rise of commercial photography galleries and the advertising-driven publications that serve them has led many commentators to decry a "death of criticism". A look at history shows that this complaint is as old as criticism itself. It is true that plenty of contemporary writing about photography is brazenly promotional. Yet new publications and platforms launch every year with a commitment to independent voices and critically engaged viewpoints. The best criticism is characterised by a persistent "itch" to change something in art, the world or both. As these conversations show, photography writers continue to manifest this activist drive.

In the introduction to his important book *Classic Essays on Photography* (1980), Alan Trachtenberg noted that the history of photography as a history of *ideas* had not yet come into focus as a field. His anthology of writings on photography played a part in gathering threads of an intellectual history for photography, including key mid-20th century texts by Walter Benjamin, Siegfried Kracauer, André Bazin, Roland Barthes and John Berger. Trachtenberg's choices were prescient; the contributors to *Writer Conversations* cite a number of those writers as enduringly influential to them. We cannot help but wonder how he could have failed to include an extract from Susan Sontag's seminal 1977 book *On Photography*, presumably because it was so recent.

Over the course of the 1970s and 80s, a canon of essential texts began to take shape on the reading lists of the photography courses that were opening up in Europe and the US. Alongside writings on photography were key critical theory texts drawn from semiotics, psychoanalysis, film theory, feminist theory, philosophy and sociology. Many of our participants cite influences from these bodies of thought including Laura Mulvey, Stuart Hall, bell hooks and Jacques Derrida. Also in this period, a generation of photographic artists and educators including Allan Sekula, Victor Burgin, Martha Rosler and John Tagg produced urgent, polemical essays about photography and its uses. These writers combined academic rigour with ethical engagement, setting a standard for future teachers and writers. The work of photography writers in this period contributed to influential cultural shifts in the representation of class, race, political violence and the AIDS crisis.

The MIT Press journal *October*, founded in 1976, provided a high-water mark for a genre of theoretically engaged academic writing about art and photography, and made a key contribution to debates around photography and postmodernism. Throughout the 1980s and 90s, *October* essays by writers such as Rosalind Krauss, Abigail Solomon-Godeau and Benjamin Buchloh were read as much in art schools as they were in art history programmes in the US and UK. Academic journals continue to support important photographic scholarship, but they no longer have the same hold on the imaginations of young makers. Some commentators argue that the momentum for new ideas in the field has shifted from art history to curation – a proposition we asked our participants to discuss. Many of the writers in our selection publish articles and books within an academic context, benefitting from specialised discourses to convey complex ideas. At the same time, several define their practice as writers in opposition to an academic mode often perceived as inaccessible or oppressive.

The abbreviated account I have provided here reflects my own trajectory through photography writing. However, our writers' responses trace many other possible pathways. The field of photography writing produced in the academic and art world centres of Europe and the US has opened up tremendously in recent years, creating the ideal conditions for this book. In the 21st century, an area of inquiry that had been overwhelmingly Western, white and male has expanded to encompass a far broader range of subject positions and approaches. Interdisciplinarity has become the norm, and photographic studies may now encompass post-colonial theory, race studies, queer studies, performance studies, forensics, ecology and more, in line with current global concerns. All the factors that have gone into creating a sense of unparalleled possibility in contemporary photography also create the broadest possible platform for photography writing that may cross genres and defy expectations.

The writers selected to respond to our questionnaire embrace this contemporary openness with a commitment to engaged, ethical writing. Some have led the transformation of the field by opening new spaces within the canon of photographic history and decolonising its discourses. As a photography historian, essayist and curator, Deborah Willis has been a pioneer in recuperating the photographs and voices of African-Americans, initiating fresh dialogues around class, race and gender. Approaching photographs as an anthropologist, Christopher Pinney has led a shift in attention from the depicted content of photographs to the ways that they are used in everyday life, a turn with great significance for image-makers as well as audiences. Art historian and curator Wu Hung has used specific case studies to draw deep meanings from the vast, under-explored history of Chinese photography.

The practices and labours of writing are themselves a recurring focus. As a curator and co-founder of *Revue Noire*, Simon Njami brings the linguistic flair of a novelist to a career of drawing African artists and urban cultures into the international spotlight. A writer whose academic calling has involved teaching art writers, David Levi Strauss highlights the labour – and difficulty – of writing responsibly. A feminist theorist of visual culture and contemporary art, Tina M. Campt underlines the importance of responding to images, and the process of writing about them, in the body and with attention to everyday lived experience. David Campany writes alongside new photography in a rich variety of modes, including conversations with prominent photographers and noted essays to accompany the exhibitions he curates.

Many of the writers illuminate specific aspects of photography or ways it is unfolding in particular parts of the world. Challenging orthodoxies, these writers propose new values for their areas of practice. An editor and curator concerned with photography and social justice, Max Houghton has contributed to the current reimagining of documentary, in part through the work of female photographers. A curator and writer, Horacio Fernández is engaged with the materiality of photography, and is particularly well known for his recuperative history of the Latin American photobook. The scholarship of art historian Olga Smith has focused on the particular dynamics of French photography and theory, regarded through the lens of a broader European perspective. An editor of the South Asian *Pix* platform, Tanvi Mishra explores the tension between insider and outsider status, along with the power dynamics inherent in being an image-maker or writer.

Some of our chosen writers explore the dangers of photography and the challenges inherent in writing. A poet, academic and advocate of slow writing, Daniel C. Blight wrestles with the problematics of writing in relation to photographic representation and whiteness. Photographic historian Taous R. Dahmani traces battles within photographic representation since the 1970s, in particular artistic practices that offer a form of insubordination. Writer and activist Zoé Samudzi works on the ethics of photography and asks us to look head-on at depictions of structural violence in the world. Others look towards the future and what role photography and writing may take in shaping our experience of it. Bridging media philosophy and critical digital practice, Joanna Zylinska challenges us to pay attention to the ways photography – so much of it now made by machines – mediates our current perception and experience. At a moment of environmental crisis, Taco Hidde Bakker asks how we can do anything that is not also an address to climate. As with many of our writers, his responses underline that an ethical approach to photography writing can also be an ethical response to important issues in the world.

Each writer received a uniform set of questions, designed to draw out the singularity of their practice. We explore their entry into the field, their individual working process, their motivations, their take on the current state of photography theory and criticism and their relationship – as both reader and writer – to other texts in the field. In most cases, the editors followed up with a small number of additional questions, designed to clarify responses or to draw out the unique perspective of the participant. As a counterpoint to the previous volume, *Curator Conversations*, we asked the writers to discuss the current relationship of photographic histories and theories to curation. The final question, about the ongoing role of criticality, underlines what is at stake for each of them. The responses that they provided are considered in relation to one another in the Afterword by Duncan Wooldridge. Many of the writers describe writing as slow, demanding, painful – even agonising! We are extremely grateful to them for giving their time to this project, and for opening their private writing process to our scrutiny.

The struggle between photographs and writing is a fruitful one in which meaning is mutually forged or foregone. What emerges from this volume is that fact that many of our leading writers share the conviction that photography writing is not merely a forum for abstract thought, self-expression or cultural play, but rather an important arena to negotiate value and meaning, and even to provoke change. It is on this premise that the *1000 Words* platform was founded in 2008, and on which the *Conversations* series was launched in 2020. We hope that this volume of *Writer Conversations* will renew your interest in photography and in writing, leading you onward to new images, new texts and new ideas.

Interviews

Tina M. Campt

Tina M. Campt is a black feminist theorist of visual culture and contemporary art. She is Owen F. Walker Professor of Humanities and Modern Culture and Media at Brown University, Providence, Rhode Island, US, where she leads the Black Visualities Initiative at the Cogut Institute for Humanities. Her early work theorised gender, racial and diasporic formation in black communities in Europe and southern Africa and the role of vernacular photography in historical interpretation. Campt is the author of Other Germans: Black Germans and the Politics of Race, Gender and Memory in the Third Reich *(University Michigan Press, 2004);* Image Matters: Archive, Photography and the African Diaspora in Europe *(Duke University Press, 2012);* Listening to Images *(Duke University Press, 2017)* and A Black Gaze *(MIT Press, 2021). She is the founding convenor of the Practicing Refusal Collective and the Sojourner Project.*

I started to write about photographs after writing my first book, which was an oral history of the Black community in Germany in the Nazi regime. I started writing about photographs of these individuals because I was asked to do a sound installation on their accounts of their life at that period of time. What forced me to actually start writing about images is that when we did the sound installation, when we were designing it and trying to think through it, what I realised is that there is no way to get people to listen to anything without giving them a focal point to look at. It was a real challenge because I had strenuously avoided including photographs of the individuals who I had spoken to, because I felt that anytime I presented my work, someone in the audience would ask: "Well, what did they look like?". "What did they look like?" became this way of indexing whether or not their account would be true, or could be true, based on how they looked, so that their race had to register in their bodies and on their faces in order for their accounts of their experiences in the Third Reich to be considered true. I had always avoided using photographs because I didn't want to put those individuals and their stories in that position. But when I faced the challenge of having people be in a sound installation and to stop to absorb it, I started looking for their photos, collecting their photos [to do that].

After that sound installation, I was just so incredibly impacted by their photographs because they resonated with me so much, even though they were of families that were very different than my own. And I started writing about the photographs in order to give voice to the responses that I was having that I couldn't explain. And it really was just an experiment because I never studied photography, art, history, any kind of visual culture in college or in graduate school. I strenuously avoided that as well, and these photographs kind of lured or tantalised me. They provoked me to try and articulate what they solicited in me, and that became a practice that, ever since I started writing, has been both terrifying and truly exhilarating.

Yes, it is. I was just reading this morning about Generation X and suddenly realised that I am Generation X! I always thought I was another generation! In this article I was reading, I recognised myself because Generation X was the generation of MTV. We were the generation where images inundated us in a way that was unfiltered. And previously there had been so many more filters on images and their circulation. So, as somebody who from childhood – I got my first television when I was six years old, a tiny, tiny Sony Trinitron that my grandmother gave me – I have been inundated with images all of my life. At the same time, that has made me someone who can easily gloss over images because I'm so used to them being such a strong part of my life. With photographs, I had the exact opposite experience, which was that I couldn't gloss over them. They grabbed me and I would just get lost in them. And so the practice that you're talking about is really about trying to linger in that experience of encounter and to share it in a way that makes others linger in the same process. So that's always been the motivation. It's always been a little bit like: "Does this image do the same thing to you as it does to me?" And I've never expected a "Yes", but the nature of my writing is to ask that question and to get people to think about the answers.

I had one practice and it's changed more recently in the last couple of years. The first writing practice was with photographs, and it was about spending some time looking at a photograph, and then putting it away and writing about what I thought I saw, or what I thought I was experiencing in relationship to it, and then bringing the photograph back and reading what I wrote while looking at the image and seeing what I got wrong or what the gaps were. My next step was not necessarily to correct the gaps, but to write about where they came from, if there was a disjuncture between what I thought I saw and what I saw. I tried to articulate why that was; so why, for example, did I think that I saw a kid that looked really happy when the kid looked really sullen? There was something about me bringing something to that image that led me down that path, and I think that's important, to not just write about images to describe them exactly. What I try and do is to describe a relationship to them that develops both through seeing and feeling, and allowing yourself to feel and respond. And so that sort of "look, look away, look, look away" was the way in which I wrote about vernacular photographs.

Since I've started writing about contemporary art and film, it's kind of changed. It's become much more physical because I rarely have the images. I'm rarely in possession of them, or I rarely have an extended period of time with them. With contemporary art, I usually sit on the floor. I sit on the floor of the museum and just literally look and write, look and write, for as long as I possibly can, before people start to make me feel uncomfortable. I then take that away and go home and continue writing. I set this intention or aspiration. The first part of that process is ethnographic: I'm sort of writing about myself encountering an image or a piece of art. And then it's about unpacking the rest of what that relationship looks like, like what are the larger contextual things? And then, more recently, I've started writing about film and that has also become this extraordinarily spatial and haptic encounter, where I usually have to set up my computer with a sound system that will allow me to have contact with the audio, because the audio and the visual are so intertwined that I need to be able to feel the sound of a film. This is much harder for moving image; it's harder to write in relationship to, and so I find it to be a really tedious process where usually I have my computer and I have an iPad and then I'm typing and I'll pause and then I keep typing. It's literally simultaneous to the moving of it, and once I get the whole thing down, I re-watch it, and then I've usually memorised the actual film by the time I'm done, and I can tell you what it is, frame by frame.

That has also shifted over time. When I first started writing about the family photographs with Black German families, what motivated me to write about them was trying to account for visual intimacy at a moment or in a circumstance where that seemed impossible. Those photographs were able to capture care, intimacy and relation in ways that I had never seen written about before. I carried that forward into writing about the vernacular images of the Black British community (the Afro-Caribbean community in Birmingham), where, in their staged photographs, I found a level of identity that was expressed so profoundly, and so profoundly beyond words.

That was a moment in time when I was thinking about "what do photographs allow people to do, or to say?" That was really the question of *Image Matters* (2012): what do they help us to do, or to say when we don't have the other resources to do or say that? When I was writing about compelled photographs, it was the same question: what do these images allow those individuals to do and to say beyond what the state is telling them to do and to say through their image making.

More recently, the question that that has motivated my writing is how does the work of contemporary artists challenge us to see our world differently and to see it by feeling our implication in some of the injustices of this current moment? Those artists' lenses – and those lenses can be cameras, can be clay, can be a stage, can be can be all sorts – give us a frame that takes us outside of ourselves and puts us in proximity with things we don't want to be in proximity with. And so the question I have had is: how do they do that? How are they able to put us in proximity to things that we don't want to be proximate to, and how does that change us in the process?

I'm a bad reader! I am the reader I tell my students not to be, which is I skim. It's a kind of excavation. I read really quickly and I'm searching for something, and when I find it, I read it over and over and over again. It becomes a wormhole. I got my PhD in History, and I was trained to be a reader of footnotes, and so I'm somebody who, once I get there, that sends me elsewhere to find all these other things. My synapses start going. And so I am both the reader that I tell my students not to be, which is to skim, and then I am who I tell them to be, which is to read openly and capaciously and connect the dots, and read people who are in conversation with each other. I tend to read in clusters.

How significant are theories and histories of photography now that curation is so prominent?

You know, the thing that is most noteworthy to me is that curation and theories and histories of photography are completely intertwined, because we are at a moment when the curators themselves are so deeply invested and so deeply conversant with those histories and theories. There's a sort of changing of the guard. I don't know if it's the same over in the UK, but in the United States over the course of the pandemic, everybody seems to be moving: curators moving from here to there to there, and there's been this reshuffle and it's exciting because so many are new curators, young curators and curators of colour – they are people who didn't come out of the art world; they come out of a world of critical theory around photography and the practice of art.

You see it in wall texts and in catalogues where the curators are referencing different theories and histories and are trying not only to put photography in conversation with genre, which used to be the way. Every curator was an Art Historian; that's what it used to be. That isn't the case anymore. It used to be that a catalogue would give you a kind of genealogy of the genre, of the form, of the content or context. And now I feel that curators are actually invoking the language of theory in order to talk about the impact of the work. They feed on one another.

The other thing is that photographers and artists are more steeped in theories of photography than they had been, and that's another ongoing conversation. I'm finding right now that one of the delights of my work is that I am being asked more and more often to be in conversation with artists, who know my work, and I know their work, and those two things are no longer separate. It used to be that the history and theory of photography used to write about photography and photographers. Now we're talking to them, and they're talking to us, and it's not an argument, it's a conversation!

The leading art schools (in the US) like Yale, RISD (Rhode Island School of Design) and Cal Arts (California Institute of the Arts) have theorists amongst them and that is recognised as valuable, and I have felt that. I do at least one art critique at the end of every semester, where somebody asks me to come to their studio class and participate in a nine-hour critique, which is exhausting but I also learn so much from that!

I always admire clarity. I admire the writer that doesn't only seek to draw you in to their writing, but also takes steps towards you in their writing. Some of the most inspirational writers to me are friends of mine, whose work has been a model and an inspiration. Christina Sharpe's work, Hazel Carby's most recent work, *Imperial Intimacies* (2019), my friend Saidiya Hartman. What they're doing is they're putting themselves in the mix, and, in doing that, they're emphasising the stakes of both what they're writing about, and how they're writing about it. The "how" becomes an intentional intervention, of: "I am going to write this to you, in a way that addresses you, which doesn't make it easier to read what I'm writing about, it raises the stakes of reading it."

That's what I really do admire, and that's what I try to do in my own writing, is to let you understand what the stakes are of both what I'm writing about and how I've chosen to write it to you. Which I hope allows you to enter it, and take certain risks as well with your own engagement.

Which texts have influenced you the most?

Some of the writers I've just mentioned. I teach (Christina Sharpe's) *In the Wake* (2016) over and over again. I teach (Saidiya Hartman's) *Wayward Lives* (2019) over and over again. I also teach Laura Mulvey. Right now, I'm in a love affair with Mulvey and Kaja Silverman: not because I absolutely agree with what they're saying, but because they open my mind every time I read them. bell hooks I teach over and over again, and I read her over and over again. Fred Moten as well. And you know who else I can't quit? Stuart Hall! Can't quit him! Ever relevant. Every time you go back to him, you really you can't believe he wrote it so long ago.

What is the place of criticality in photography writing now?

I hate to answer a question with a question but it really does depend on where that photography writing is. One thing I've been noticing is that there's a lot more general writing about photography, in newspapers and in reviews, in daily circulating publications, and I don't find that critical very often. But again, I feel like criticality has taken a front seat in the art world, amongst curators, amongst this entire Third Estate that's no longer journalism. So I guess it's a Fourth Estate, which is the critical commentary that you get in blogs and in podcasts and on social media, because the general public is at a point right now where they feel empowered to critique and to critique photography in particular. I think that's also because of the role of photography in documenting the horrible state that the world is in right now, be that on race relations and social justice, or the pandemic, or immigration, or housing. Those images are mobilising and, at the same time, they are documenting certain kinds of injustice. (They record) not only the acts of injustice, but the acts of injustice that the camera perpetrates as well. So it has become this invitation to a broader form of criticality than used to be prevalent.

I wondered whether you could talk a little about the
importance of everyday experience in relation to your
writing. Your writing reveals how a seemingly modest
image contains so much possibility and all that it
starts to bring into being. Your writing is drawn to
the necessity of thinking through everyday experience,
and its representation.

The importance of the everyday, for me, is that our most intense struggles occur in the everyday. There is a desire in me to be accountable not to the extraordinary, but to the ordinary. And when we're accountable to the ordinary, then we are valuing the experiences of those who rarely get much attention. When you ask about its significance to me, I think that's how we learn practices of survival. We don't learn practices of survival in the extraordinary circumstances of a car crash or a plane crash, or being marooned on an island. We develop these strategies incrementally over time. That's what I see in everyday photography and vernacular photography. When I come to those images, I'm always asking how did we get here, and what is it that connects us to mundane images: in their mundane-ness, you find these jewels, these jewels of love, of kindness, of generosity, of care. And you find the flip side too. You find the quotidian violences that are also brought to bear. There's this image in *Image Matters* that I try to take apart, of a woman on a table in a corner. When you take it apart you realise that she's in a gynaecologist office and there's a procedure that happened or didn't happen. Every woman has been in that situation, but to have an everyday photograph of it, an anonymous one... When I saw it at an exhibition, I just stopped in my tracks. It's not because it was exceptional, it's because it was so ordinary. We can illuminate so much about our lives by lingering in relationship to the ordinary and thinking about how we survive it and how countless other people survive it as well.

Listening to Images *made me conscious of how the stakes
are there in the image of the everyday. Perhaps this is
what's most resisted by positions of power? They are the
most essential images in a sense, to just be seen, to be
seen to be living, to be loving, to be sharing.*

That is one of the tricks of ideology: to highlight the exceptional as that which you are supposed to be striving to be or become. That then becomes this impossible striving towards something you can never accomplish. And it keeps you in your place. But when you value who you are, it becomes a powerful source of identification and affirmation. And that's my resistance to the exceptional: I don't want to be exceptional. I want to share a world with others where we have some sense of equivalence. I think that's a beautiful world, as opposed to the one where there are some who are exceptional and others who are not.

David Levi Strauss

David Levi Strauss is the author of Co-illusion: Dispatches from the End of Communication *(MIT Press, 2020);* Photography and Belief *(David Zwirner Books, 2020, and in an Italian edition by Johan & Levi, 2021);* Words Not Spent Today Buy Smaller Images Tomorrow *(Aperture, 2014);* In Case Something Different Happens in the Future: Joseph Beuys and 9/11 *(Documenta 13, 2012);* From Head to Hand: Art and the Manual *(Oxford University Press, 2010),* Between the Eyes: Essays on Photography and Politics, *with an introduction by John Berger (Aperture, 2003, 2012 and in an Italian edition by Postmedia Books, 2007) and* Between Dog & Wolf: Essays on Art and Politics *(Autonomedia, 1999 and 2010).*

He has also co-edited To Dare Imagining: Rojava Revolution, *with Michael Taussig, Peter Lamborn Wilson and Dilar Dirik (Autonomedia, 2016, and in an Italian edition by Elèuthera, 2017) and* The Critique of the Image Is the Defense of the Imagination, *with Strauss, Taussig and Wilson (Autonomedia, 2020). From 2007–21, Strauss directed the graduate programme in Art Writing at the School of Visual Arts, New York, US.*

In 1975, when I was a 22-year-old poet, I went to study photography with Nathan Lyons at Visual Studies Workshop, which, at that time, was the best photography school in the US. MIT Press had just published Nathan's landmark book of photographs, *Notations in Passing* (1971). When I first attended Nathan's seminar, I handed him a handwritten copy of an essay I'd written in response to *Notations in Passing*, titled "The Ontology of the Eye, or A Stall of Cows, A Stall of Images". It began this way: 'The eye cannot be separated from the brain or memory. Visual data, like all sensory data, are immediately plugged into the complex mega-memory of the brain/soul.' The other students in the seminar thought this was the most impertinent act they'd ever witnessed, but Nathan liked the piece. That was the beginning.

What is your writing process?

My process is ridiculously labour intensive and inefficient. I write 50 pages to get a page. I first produce an unwieldly mass of language, and then carve it down. It takes an incredibly long time. It's a sculptural process, from the inside-out. I use montage and magic. The first sentence usually comes last.

It feels like there is something very photographic about this, the quantity of writing and the carefully selected final outcome, its compulsive recording and intensive editing. In the same way that a photographer develops a series of strategies, shortcuts and go-tos, are there tools or strategies that facilitate your final montage? How do you know that writing reaches the stage where you can write that first sentence?

I've never thought about my writing process having a correlative in photography, but I think you're right. It is a process of selection. Each word is chosen from a very large number of possibilities, and, when each word is chosen, it affects every other word around it. The larger currents that determine form are rhythm and rhyme, at the level of phrase, clause, sentence and paragraph. If you get too attached to the individual words, you lose the music, and, if you lose the music, you lose the reader.

In the end, you've got to be able to separate yourself from the writing, and look at it as if someone else wrote it. Only then can you get to that level of absolute ruthlessness that is necessary in rewriting.

For me, the process is endless. At a certain point, someone takes it away from me and then it's done. Like Duke Ellington said: "I don't need time. What I need is a *deadline*."

What are the questions or problems that motivate your writing?

I write to find out what I think about things. I try to focus on the persistent questions: Why are we here? What does it mean? How and why do we believe technical images the way we do? How do these images actually work? Who benefits from this?

Right now, I'm trying to write about the End of the World, and the first question is: What is the world? This puts me immediately back at the image of the world. Most of the questions I deal with send me back to the image.

Something really distinctive in your recent writing is the way that images not only record the world but are informing it, producing it even. And your writing, dialogically, seems to want to change the image in turn. Do you write in order to challenge, and even change what the image might be?

Yes, absolutely. I want to change the image of the world, in however limited a way I can, through enactment and persuasion. One of the biggest problems in our time is that we no longer have a viable social image of the world.

What kind of reader are you?

I've been a driven, voracious reader since I first learned to read, before starting grade school, and that has never changed. I read to live. When I was a child, my father discouraged me from reading, and sometimes punished me for it, thinking that it was an excuse not to work. So, I read in secret, sometimes literally in the closet and under the sheets. The act of reading always felt illicit to me, and this feeling never really went away. When I began to be encouraged to read in

school, I always thought someone, surely, would realise that what
I was doing was wrong, that I could go anywhere and be anyone
when I read, and those in charge would realise how dangerous this
was and stop me, but no one ever did.

*How significant are theories and histories of photography
now that curation is so prominent?*

More significant than ever, I think. Photographic images are a
significant part of the mechanism of social control in the world today,
and we need to understand how they work and where they came from
in order to resist this control.
  I taught from 2001–05 at the Center for Curatorial Studies at Bard
College, New York, and I became dismayed by the prevalence of what
I came to call "curatorial rhetoric"; writing that borrowed terms and
concepts from various specialised languages and used this jargon to
protect the writer, and the reader, from experiencing the art in
question. When I despaired of getting curators to abandon this kind
of prophylactic rhetoric, I began to encourage them to hire outside
writers, instead, to write catalogue essays.

*You were Chair of the School of Visual Arts in New York's
celebrated Art Writing programme until very recently,
overlapping with your time at Bard. In what ways did
teaching writing inform your own practice?*

By the time I became Chair of the Art Writing programme, I had been
writing seriously for over 30 years, and had already gone through
many transformations. But teaching certainly made me more aware
of the difficulties and the dilemmas of writing in the present,
as experienced by my younger students.
  Teaching is a fundamentally optimistic act, like writing. In both,
you're imagining your reader/student into existence – imagining the
very best of them. And I've been extremely lucky to have so many
of my students join in this mutually transformative act.

What qualities do you admire in other writers?

Courage, honesty, generosity, risk and kindness.

The writings of John Berger, Walter Benjamin, Susan Sontag, Paul Virilio, Vilém Flusser, Jacques Ellul, Edward Said, Aimé Césaire, Albert Camus, Paul Valéry, Hannah Arendt, Simone Weil, Marsilio Ficino, Leo Steinberg, Leon Golub, Jimmie Durham, Amiri Baraka, Linda Nochlin, Lucy Lippard, Elena Poniatowska, Guy Davenport, James Baldwin, Flann O'Brien, Samuel Beckett, Peter Lamborn Wilson, Michael Taussig, William Burroughs, Paul Bowles, Jean Genet and Pier Paolo Pasolini.

And the poetry and prose of Arthur Rimbaud, Charles Baudelaire, John Keats, William Blake, Ezra Pound, William Carlos Williams, H.D., Charles Olson, Robert Duncan, Robin Blaser, Diane di Prima and many others in this lineage.

What is the place of criticality in photography writing now?

The more pressing question is: What is the place of criticality, or critical thinking, in the social realm today? Our current communications environment has reduced critical thinking to personal preferences and opinions, and amplified anger and fear, and that has made it difficult to engage difficult questions in the larger social frame with criticality. We need to find new ways to talk about important things.

Joanna Zylinska

Joanna Zylinska is an artist, writer, curator and Professor of Media Philosophy + Critical Digital Practice at King's College London. She is an author of a number of books, including AI Art: Machine Visions and Warped Dreams *(Open Humanities Press, 2020) and* Nonhuman Photography *(MIT Press, 2017). She also co-edited open-access works,* Photomediations: An Open Book *and* Photomediations: A Reader, *as part of the Europeana Space project funded by the European Commission.*

Zylinska's art practice involves experimenting with different kinds of image-based media. In 2013, she served as Artistic Director of Transitio_MX05 Biomediations, the biggest Latin American new media festival, which took place in Mexico City. She is currently researching perception and cognition as boundary zones between human and machine intelligence, whilst trying to answer the question: 'Does photography have a future?'.

I came to writing about photography (rather than just photographs) relatively late in my career. I had been working as a media academic at Goldsmiths, University of London, teaching the philosophical and cultural aspects of digital media for many years. I had also had an active research interest in art, particularly new media art. But photography had been my secret love, something I had practiced "on the side", so to speak, but that I hadn't brought into any of my more "proper" academic work. It all changed in 2007, when, still working at Goldsmiths, I decided to enrol on a practice-based MA in photography at the University of Westminster. I did that a little bit in secret too! Doing that MA changed everything. It encouraged me to start incorporating practice into my written work, to change the way I write and to address photography more comprehensively as a key medium of our times. It also led me to develop a new philosophy of photography, culminating in my book, *Nonhuman Photography* (2017). (Analysing photographs that were not *of*, *by* or *for* the human, that book looked at the photographic medium across the scale of so-called 'deep time'. It positioned various 'impressioning' practices, from fossils through to tanning, as forms of photographic practice, alongside its more conventional forms such as photograms, analogue film frames or digital snapshots.)

What is your writing process?

Because I try to maintain that dual track of having an image-based practice as well as working on photography philosophically, I am very mindful that writing about photography shouldn't use photographs just as illustrations. Rather, in recognition of photography's agency, I would say that I write *with* photographs. Often these will be projects by other people (artworks, social media practices) or social and technical networks in which photographs play an active role (Internet search engines, image databases for training AI algorithms). But I also try to develop some aspects of my theoretical argument *from* photographic practice. So I often start with an idea *and* a project – like with *Active Perceptual Systems*, where I wore a necklace-like Autographer camera for two years whilst writing about nonhuman vision, or when I hired workers from Amazon's Mechanical Turk labour platform to take a photo from the window of the room they were in with a view to creating a collective portrait of invisible 'undigital' global workforce, as part of my work on AI and art. So, in my work, I try to get writing and image-based practice to speak to each other, to push each other and then also, inevitably, to converge.

The primary concern of my work over the years has been the constitution of the human as both a species and a historical subject. Adopting this geological probe of 'deep time' mentioned earlier, I have looked at the emergence of the human in conjunction with the surrounding technologies, such as tools and other artefacts but also communication in its various modes – be it everyday language, storytelling, ethics, art and, last but not least, photography. In an attempt to challenge human exceptionalism without giving up on my own curiosity about my phylogenetic kin (i.e., other people), in my writing, I zoom in on the signal points of the human such as intelligence, consciousness and perception. With this, I aim to explore the entanglements of human and nonhuman forms of intelligence, including the promises and threats offered by AI and machine vision. Currently, I am working on perception as arguably the key mode of engagement with the world in different species. This project involves looking at the reconfiguration of 'the eye' in the digital age and at the humanist blind spot in machine vision. As part of this work, I am investigating the role played by images, especially mechanically-produced images such as photographs, in human becoming. Looking at the transformation of photography by computation – and the transformation of human perception by algorithmically-driven images, from CGI to AI – I am also trying to figure out what it means to live surrounded by image flows and machine eyes. This radical transformation of the photographic medium is currently leading me to explore a question which is also a provocation: 'Does photography have a future?'

My work is produced from within the theoretical standpoint recognised as critical posthumanism, a position that does not mean any straightforward overcoming of the human (were such a thing even possible), but that rather involves a rewriting or re-enactment of the human under the conditions of the planetary crisis resulting from the nexus of colonialism, globalisation, technoscience, late capitalism and climate change. You could say that I'm trying to *write myself out* of the conceptual and political strictures of humanism, with its constitutive forms of violence. I'm trying to accomplish this both in the content of my writings and in its style – which is often hesitant, minimal as well as ironic. This attempt also involves mixing different genres, different modes of enquiry and different media. At the same time, I'm aware that, even though many animals are known to leave traces – i.e. surface marks which could be seen as forms of inscription – grammatological writing is a specifically human practice; a practice that both makes sense to and is valued by humans. So, I'm also writing in full recognition of writing being a species-specific behaviour to which we humans have assigned a particular cultural value (a value which I of course also hold dear).

My work, both written and image-based, is indeed produced within the horizon of extinction, which represents the awareness of the eventual expiration of the human species and other species alongside us, and of our planet as a whole. But it's also driven by a sense of urgency prompted by the foreshortening of this horizon as a result of the destructive human impact on planet Earth. Photography has of course been part of this impact – from the extraction of minerals needed to produce cameras and the use of harmful photochemical materials through to photography's participation in the extractive data economy which is extremely resource-heavy (even if it's sold to us through images of immaterial flows and clouds). Yet photography, as you point out, has also been used to represent, record and challenge practices leading to this accelerated extinction. Last but not least, there's an existential dimension to photography for me. Photography, a *par excellence* practice of imaging and imagination (i.e. a practice of copying, making likenesses, mapping, making mental pictures and

ideating), can serve as a conduit for asking bigger questions about
our own 'thrownness' in the world – of which we are only temporary
inhabitants – and of imagining different futures for ourselves and our
planet. This future-oriented horizon of extinction, beyond the death
of singular humans (be it that of Roland Barthes' mother or our own),
makes photography into what Swedish philosopher Amanda
Lagerkvist has called 'an existential medium'.

What kind of reader are you?

Committed, engaged, playful – but also forgetful. You could say that
I read for an experience of an idea rather than for the purpose of
constructing world systems out of the previously existing ideas.

*How significant are theories and histories of photography
now that curation is so prominent?*

My previous answer might signify that I don't care much about
historical unfoldings and coherent linear trajectories. But this couldn't
be further from the truth. I recognise that meaningful photographic
curation requires expertise, which needs to involve familiarity with
theories and histories of photography. We also have to remember that
these theories and histories are already forms of curation – and that
they can be rewritten, restaged, rearranged.

What qualities do you admire in other writers?

A mixture of rigour and vitality and a desire to say something
interesting and new about the world. I appreciate writers who have
an awareness of their own writerly task – and who take this task (but
not necessarily themselves, under the guise of 'Here I Am as a Great
Writer Speaking to You My Dear Reader') seriously. My ideal writerly
voice would be Roland Barthes from *A Lover's Discourse* (1977) –
but not, for the love of God, *Camera Lucida* (1980) – hybridised with
Donna Haraway and Rebecca Solnit, and then remixed through some
postcolonial epistemologies and affects, such as those coming from
Eduardo Viveiros de Castro.

What texts have influenced you the most?

There are so many – from texts on photography by writers such as Vilém Flusser, Geoffrey Batchen and Tina M. Campt, through to those whose authors have shown me the way with words and concepts: Jacques Derrida, Hélène Cixous, Tim Ingold, Juhani Pallasmaa, Stanisław Lem. The book I wish I had written myself is *Pandora's Camera: Photogr@phy After Photography* (2014) by Joan Fontcuberta.

What is the place of criticality in photography writing now?

We now live in image flows – we are surrounded by photographs on screens large and small, and are mediating our relationships with others through images. Photographs and other images form a transparent layer through which we see the world. I am increasingly concerned about the fact that this layer remains largely unseen. So, for me, the function of criticality in photography writing would consist in drawing attention to that seemingly transparent photographic layer, to see it for what it is, for what it's made of and for how it's made. This would need to involve going beyond semiotic readings of individual images – although I believe there is still need for developing an image literacy of an interpretative kind. But it would also need to involve developing an understanding of image infrastructures and of the way those infrastructures are involved in shaping our socio-political reality today. With this, we could perhaps go so far as to argue not only that photography writing needs to include criticality but also that *any* form of critical theory and critical writing today needs to engage, seriously and profoundly, with photography.

Simon Njami

Simon Njami is an independent curator, lecturer, art critic and novelist. He studied at Sorbonne, Paris, France, and was the Co-Founder and Editor-in-Chief of Revue Noire. He served as Artistic Director of Johannesburg Art Fair (2008), the Bamako Photography Biennale and the Dak'Art Biennale (2016–18). He has occupied roles at the World Press Photo Awards, and co-curated the first African Pavilion at the 52nd Venice Biennale. He is the President of the International Festival of Extraordinary Textiles.

Njami has curated numerous exhibitions of contemporary art and photography, including Africa Remix (2004–07), African Art Fair (Johannesburg, South Africa, 2008); The Divine Comedy (SCAD Museum of Art Savannah, Georgia, US and Museum für Moderne Kunst, Frankfurt, Germany, 2014; The Smithsonian, Washington DC, US, 2015); Xenopolis (Deutsche Bank KunstHalle, Berlin, Germany, 2015); After Eden, The Artur Walther Collection (Maison Rouge, Paris, 2015); Afriques Capitales (Paris and Lille, France, 2017); Metropolis (MAXXI, Rome, Italy, 2018); I is another (Galleria Nazionale d'Arte Moderna e Contemporanea, Rome, 2018); Aujourd'hui (National Museum of Cameroon, Yaoundé, 2019); The Studio (Kampala Art Biennale, Uganda, 2019); This space between us (Centro Atlántico de Arte Moderno, Las Palmas, Spain, 2020) and Materia Prima (Galleria Continua, San Giminiano, Italy, 2021).

Njami served as a Visiting Professor at University of San Diego, California, US between 1991–93. In 1998, he created the Pan African masterclasses in photography with the Goethe Institut, and set up the collection of contemporary art for the Memorial ACTe, Pointe-à-Pitre, Guadeloupe. He created, and is conducting, the workshop AtWork with the Moleskine Foundation. He is the author of biographies on James Baldwin and Leopold Sédar Senghor and four novels.

I published my first novel when I was 23. I was always fascinated by the difference between photography (which is a process) and "reality". As far as writing about photography itself is concerned, from what I recall, philosophers such as Jean-Paul Sartre, Edmund Husserl and Maurice Merleau-Ponty who reflected on the notion of image opened my curiosity. Novelists such as Mikhail Bulgakov or Marcel Proust, to name a few, also played their role. Therefore, photography as such was not, at the beginning, my first interest, but rather the notion of representation, perception and incarnation.

What is your writing process?

I start by looking at the photograph, in a kind of clinical manner. The frame, the lighting, the focus… Then I try to compare what the photographers' intentions are compared to what I see. At last, I look for a word that would trigger a process of analysis.

You work and write across languages and cultures. Do you have any reflections on writing for the Anglosphere versus a Francophone context? Are there embedded properties of language or patterns of thought that strike you as impacting the discussion of photography in different ways? My own sense is that, in French, the relationship between literary and academic/critical writing may be more fluid. Does this ring true for you?

Hegel once wrote that we think through words, and I tend to agree. I am fascinated by what I call the "idiomatic" – that is, what cannot be translated. When I write in English, I have the feeling of having less space to play. Less space to engage in a fight with words and make them say things they would not want to say. The German philosophers would create words in order to express, as accurately as possible, what they meant. French has more poetry and more organic philosophy which equals literature. There are things I can write in French that would require an extensive translation. I was told that I was a nightmare for my English translators because they are never sure of the nuance I am bringing into a sentence. I love polysemy and paradoxes. I have the feeling that I am more "straight to the point" in English. I was trained in the European way of thinking, from the Greeks to the Germans and the French.

Representation and point of view. Photography is never objective. For me, whatever photograph is produced equals a self-portrait, be it a landscape, a war image, a documentary or an essay. The photographer, whether they would admit it or not always wants to tell us a particular story. They manipulate us in order for us to see through their gaze. I am always questioning (not necessarily in a negative manner) the motivations (aesthetic, political, social) behind the image. Roland Barthes wrote somewhere about the "noisy" images that he opposed to the silent ones. I am always trying, when I see a photograph, to get rid of the noise.

Urbanity is something quite specific. It is, in my view, the cradle of modernity. It proceeds through signs, in the phenomenological point of view. A sign equals a phenomenon, which represents an event without sense. A city is a sign forger but those signs, that we can retrieve in any cities are encoded. You need a "translation" to make them intelligible to the greater number. Our aim, with *Revue Noire*, was to describe contemporaneity as a universal language spoken in local tongues. You don't write about a process the same way as you write about history. People like Guillaume Apollinaire were pivotal for their time, because they belonged. They were not acting as observers but as actors. This is why they could translate so well their comrades' productions. I have always been fascinated by translation. Not only in the linguistic sense of it, but in all its cultural and sociological aspects.

I am a critical reader, even when reading novels. It is always a discussion, a dialogue. I engage with the writer as if he was a partner on a roundtable or a friendly discussion. At times, I take notes, when something is interesting or when I face an analysis that I find particularly bold or stupid.

How significant are theories and histories of photography now that curation is so prominent?

Theories are always as interesting as history. We don't have to invent what has already been written or thought. But as Gilles Deleuze once put it, a theory must work (which means must be applied) and should that not be the case, the theoretician and his theories become useless. I think curating is applying theories and renewing them by practice. A decent curator must be a decent theoretician.

What qualities do you admire in other writers?

Intelligence, brilliance, simplicity and accuracy.

What texts have influenced you the most?

As far as photography texts are concerned, *Camera Lucida* (1980) by Barthes and *On Photography* (1977) by Susan Sontag. But in a wider scope, philosophy and literature are very important for me.

What is the place of criticality in photography writing now?

I don't know. Most of the texts I come across are mostly dealing with photography. I think photography is far beyond photography. People who restrict themselves in a kind of semiology of the images are limited in their reflections. Photography tells so much more: it contains history, art, geography, politics and so on. It is a world in itself. A space where you deal with heterotopia, heterology and heterochrony, all of which are, in my opinion, the three unique tools to read the world.

Taous R. Dahmani

Taous R. Dahmani is a French, British and Algerian art historian, writer and curator specialising in photography based between London and Marseille, France. Her projects explore the relationships between photography and politics, such as the visual culture of protests, migratory narratives and intersectional feminist discourses. Dahmani is also the content editor for the annual publication The Eyes, *a trustee of the Photo Oxford Festival and on the editorial board of* MAI: Visual Culture and Feminism. *Dahmani also served as the curator of the Louis Roederer Discovery Award at Les Rencontres d'Arles 2022, France.*

Recent writings include "Polareyes: A Magazine by and for Black British Women Photographers as a Site of Resistance in London, 1987" in Resist, Organize, Build *(SUNY Press, 2022); "Heeding time: reviewing and rereading Périphérique" in Mohamed Bourouissa,* Périphérique *(Loose Joints, 2021); "A meeting between the thought of Stuart Hall and the films of John Akomfrah" in* Penser avec Stuart Hall *(La Dispute, 2021); "Racism and anti-racist struggles in 1970s London: When the walls speak, placards respond!" in* Le phototexte engagé – Une culture visuelle du militantisme au XXe siècle *(Les Presses du réel, 2021); "From a space of resistance, to the institution's place: the history of Autograph ABP, between 1988 and 2007" in* Marges #33 *(2021) and "Bharti Parmar's True Stories: Against the grain of Sir Benjamin Stone's Photographic Collection" in* PhotoResearcher #30 *(2018).*

Dahmani is currently collaborating with photographer Joy Gregory on the publication of the first critical anthology of Black women photographers active in the UK in the 1980s and 90s, entitled Shining Lights *(MACK/ Autograph, 2023).*

The very first time I wrote about a photograph was eight years ago in a university exam for my history of photography course. We had three hours to write a "dissertation" – a methodology-heavy French way of writing a "paper". And it was actually the last time I wrote anything with a pen. I only vaguely remember that I wrote about a Bill Owens photograph and its relation to capitalism. But I vividly remember my eagerness and nascent aspiration.

Fast forward slightly less than a decade and I'm now writing up my PhD as the end product of my journey in French academia. Looking back, this education – its numerous rules and regulations – was a process of acculturation. One way of writing, to perpetuate one way of thinking. On scholarly work, Edward Said wrote that it is an 'on-going activity within an already constituted field of discourse.' It exists only to be perpetuated as it is.

In 2019, when Tim Clark, Editor in Chief of 1000 Words, invited me to write about a photobook, I welcomed the invitation as a breath of fresh air. I also welcomed the proposal as an opportunity to transcribe, for a wider readership – a conscious reasoning – the accumulation of knowledge and experience that has shaped me as a researcher. This experience started my interest in non-academic writing – its forms and meanings – and its potential for accessibility. As such, this experience was another "first time".

Today, I feel like I'm playing a tug of war with myself: one team trying to follow presiding ways of writing a PhD thesis; the other exploring the freedom of essay writing. At the end of a long and laborious project such as a PhD thesis, I am embracing the feeling of re-starting, re-becoming an apprentice writer. Originating from the French verb "essayer" (to try), "the essay" is a great form for critical thinking, and I will attempt to weave my academic background into this new form in the future – asking myself, as Daniel C. Blight asked himself a few years ago: 'What is the politics of essay writing on photography?' Blending disciplinary disregard and acute consideration for this form.

[I'll answer this question for essay writing only.]

On good days:

1. I place my phone behind my computer screen – on airplane mode – and have a cuppa to hand.
2. I put on my earphones with the curious "focus music" which populates YouTube and which helps me create a sort of "concentration bubble".
3. I read something: either from the digital pile of PDFs under my "research" folder or from an article I have received in one of the many newsletters that arrive every day in my inbox. Reading gets me focused but reading also produces two things: quotations and ideas.
4. I jot down reflections about a selected quote. In her book *In the Wake* (2016), Christina Sharpe points out that: 'thinking needs care.' I consider quotations a profound demonstration of care for thinkers and their ideas: they are "thank-yous" to the people who produced knowledge before us. They are also invitations for curious readers: footnotes open never-ending "reading pathways".
5. The accumulation of quotes and notes – and sometimes interviews with photographers – form my "base". When I'm not rushed by a deadline I let the reading, the note taking and the "base creation" percolate. The longer the better, the essay will "live" and "evolve" in my mind, creating new possible directions.
6. When the deadline is approaching, I start a new Word document and write a first draft "from scratch". The first sentence takes courage, the second trust. I can't start writing an essay if I don't have a clear orientation – often found during the "percolating period". I tend to think that essays need to make a point, be a demonstration not a decoration. But, might not the best one be precisely both?
7. I go back to my "base" to "feed" the first draft of the essay. I add precision. Because of which kind of photographs/photographers I am writing about, I am wary of ambiguity or obscurity. I make sure any complex ideas mentioned are mobilised in an intelligible way: I want to make sure they are accessible and in accordance with the assumed readership.
8. I think and write in French and English. Early drafts of most of my texts are written in both languages which ultimately leads to me feeling sorry for myself when something "comes out" fine in one language but doesn't translate well. Often, this kickstarts a

process where I juggle between a French-English dictionary
and a Thesaurus. Another challenge of writing in both these
languages is having to navigate different levels of "discourse
acceptance": concepts and ideas are not similarly established
in different countries; references and words might need to be
explained differently (especially in the fields of critical race theory
and postcolonial studies).

9.   I remove the earphones to read the paragraph written out loud,
I correct and I rectify. I repeat the process as many times as there
are paragraphs. This list was read at least five times.

On bad days:

> I generally love listening to podcasts or watching interviews of
> people who talk in detail about their craft and practice. So, on
> bad days, I turn to writers who have written about writing. I often
> think of this Marguerite Duras quote: 'One cannot write without
> bodily strength. One must be stronger than oneself to approach
> writing; one must be stronger than what one is writing.'

*What are the questions or problems that motivate your
writing?*

The last five years of my life have been dedicated to my doctoral
research. My thesis is articulated, in a nutshell, around the
photographic representation of struggles and the struggle for
photographic representation in England from the end of the 1960s to
the end of the '80s. Most of my essays, so far, have been more or less
inspired by my ongoing obsession with image-making and political
action whether expressed in iconographies or ecosystems (or 'worlds'
to reference Howard S. Becker).

That said, most of my essays have been dedicated to very
contemporary artists/photographers and, as such, most of them have
tried to "respond" to image-makers that *create dangerously* to quote
Edwidge Danticat, who describes that process as such: '[It] is creating
as a revolt against silence, creating when both the creation and the
reception, the writing and the reading, are dangerous undertakings,
disobedience to a directive.' I'm motivated by disobedient artists-
photographers. I'm driven by the problems defiant image-makers
highlight. Their insubordination can be found in their craft or form,

in their practice or discourse. They are oppositional in their way of behaving with, around or against photography. Their rebellion can be loud or whispered – I'll listen.

As a doctoral researcher, reading is a great part of my day-to-day work. As such, libraries become toolboxes and books instruments towards the completion of a project. The Stakhanovic nature of a PhD means that I rarely re-read books – with the significant exception of bell hooks whom I could read every day. If I re-read an article, it is often in order to "double check" or "make sure".

However, the first lockdown taught me the power of re-reading and reading several books at the same time: realising that, often, as with a person, you need the "right time" to truly discover a book's content. To take an example, I had always "used" Roland Barthes' theories (and taught *Camera Lucida* (1980) in exactly the same way it had been passed down by my professor), but, with my recent dive into essay writing, I started paying attention to the confidentiality, familiarity and sensitive nature of his work: making him a thousand times more interesting.

So, as I'm trying to become another kind of writer, I'm becoming another kind of reader: trying to find the route towards an embodied strategy of narration that exists at the meeting place of gut (biography) and brain (history/theory). A delicate balance between decency and intelligibility. I have to say that I have come a long way: French academic education forbids expressions of subjectivity or opinion – or more exactly, uses objectivity to hide the dominants' point of views. The first time I wrote "I" to start a sentence I felt a blast of freedom on my keyboard. In *How to Suppress Women's Writing* (1983), Johanna Russ wrote: 'Although crammed with facts and references, [women's writing] has the wrong style; it is personal and sounds unscholarly, a charge often levelled at modern feminist writing. That is, the tone is not impersonal, detached, and dry enough – in short, not patriarchal enough – to produce belief." As you can imagine, reading beacons such as Saidiya V. Hartman, Sharpe and Tina M. Campt for the first time was extremely arresting.

I struggle with this question. For me, one can only compare similar elements and the contrast between the experience of reading and the experience of visiting an exhibition is too dissimilar: providing disparate bodily and intellectual experiences. Being a reader and being a viewer/spectator are two distinct positions. However, I guess we could maybe examine the knowledge produced by catalogues vs. magazines, journals and other sorts of publications. Such an investigation might quickly lead us back to accessibility (price, printed/online, language, themes, etc.). The performative aspect of exhibitions – if the work of going through the doors of a gallery/museum is achieved – makes it probably more approachable. In the age of social media, we face very different ethics of attention and, as a result, disparate receptions/reactions/effects.

That said, if I really have to answer the question, I would say that the "prominent" status of exhibitions over theories/histories that you seem to detect is probably only the result of radical and forward-thinking theorists and historians. Good exhibitions are made by curators (and artists) who read. I have a hard time imagining the act of thinking – or giving shape to ideas – without writing, so I'm guessing curation is another form of writing. Curating can then become a translation and even a visual/embodied comment on theories/histories. Exhibitions can be powerful rhetorical demonstrations. Yet, the limitations of exhibition-making are much more real than the limits of words on paper (publication aside). For me, the main question is who writes and who curates and which platforms these people are given. *How* we know what we know and *who* is allowed to share what they know?

What qualities do you admire in other writers?

This is an extremely hard question. But to answer, I would say 1. their politics 2. their attention to detail 3. their humanity.

1.   Marguerite Duras wrote that writing is: 'Screaming without sound'. When I read Hartman, Hannah Arendt, Ariella Aïcha Azoulay, Etel Adnan and Trinh T. Minh-ha, I hear their screams. If anger is pain with nowhere to go, writing then becomes a sort of socially accepted "place". Political anger translated into words is definitely something I admire in these writers. I would also like to mention a young generation of badass writers such as Legacy Russell and her *Glitch Feminism* manifesto (2020) or Durga

Chew-Bose's singular writing in *Too Much and Not the Mood* (2017).

2.   A focus on a detail, such as a cup of coffee let's say, can be a powerful rhetorical node, as revealed beautifully by Mahmoud Darwish in *Memory for Forgetfulness* (1982). I'm not a very patient person, and struggle with the exercise of description, so, recently, when I read *A Black Gaze* (2021) by Campt, I was quite mesmerised by the attention she seems to give to descriptions of the art works she mobilises (the same consideration/scrutiny can be found in *Listening to Images* (2017) for example). A detail can also be an anecdote that becomes a compelling argument. In the same book, Campt explains the effect of the weather on her experience of an exhibition: this opened many threads of thought.

3.   I'm a big reader of autobiographies and in-depth interviews because of the possibility of hearing the artists' voices. But, the ability of writers such as Olivia Laing, for example, to emphasise her own and artists' human experiences is definitely something I admire. I never thought I would care so much about someone like Andy Warhol until I read *The Lonely City* (2016). I also love artists such as Coco Fusco who write about other artists – they tend to reveal a very distinctive perspective on the artworks they write about. I like books that are accounts of being and guides for becoming. I also like writers, who are not "writers" as such: recently I read a text written by a photographer, for the first time, wrote about a decade of work. Vasantha Yogananthan's essay, in his latest photobook *Amma* (2021), moved me greatly because of his bravery in writing about his journey as a photographer with the most generous vulnerability.

What texts have influenced you the most?

[Influence seems like a big word, but, off the top of my head, here is a non-exhaustive list of names, in no particular order, with endless recognition for carrying me through years of doctoral research.]

Edwidge Danticat Jacques Rancière Gayatri Spivak Marie-José Mondzain Allan Sekula Frantz Fanon W.J.T Mitchell Fred Moten James Baldwin Shawn Michelle Smith John Berger Paul Ricoeur Susan Sontag Sara Ahmed Stuart Hall Judith Burtler Simon de Beauvoir Eric Hazan Julia Kristeva Angela Y. Davis Adrienne Rich Nicholas Mirzoeff Edouard Glissant Christina Sharpe Elsa Tamara Trodd Dorlin Jo

Spence Sarah Lewis Victor Burgin Kobena Mercer Laura Mulvey Chris
Kraus Steve Edwards Lucy R. Lippard Val Williams Elvan Zabunyan
Mieke Bal Jacqueline Bobo Hazel V. Carby Eddie Chambers Patricia
Hill Collins Sandra Harding Elizabeth Edwards Anna Backman Rogers
Siona Wilson Harriet Riches Paul Gilroy bell hooks Heidi Safia Mirza
Griselda Pollock Rozsika Parker Liz Wells Deborah Willis Pratibha
Parmar David A. Bailey Roshini Kempadoo Sarat Maharaj Gilane
Tawados Ambalavaner Sivanandan Maurice Berger John Tagg Albert
Memmi Saul Alinsky Antonio Gramsci Audre Lorde C.L.R. James
Edward Said Homi K. Bhabha Fatima Mernissi Walter Rodney Achille
Mbembe Frieda Ekotto Derek Walcott Patrick Chamoiseau Mahmoud
Darwish Paul B. Preciado Tina M. Campt Saidiya Hartman Hannah
Arendt Ariella Aïcha Azoulay Etel Adnan Aruna D'Souza Teju Cole Trinh
T. Minh-ha and *many* others that I'll regret not naming once this
interview is published.

*What is the place of criticality in photography writing
now?*

I am tempted to give a somewhat literal answer to this question:
addressing geography and platforms. The hegemony of the English
language and concomitantly the predominance of the global North
in knowledge *dissemination* (not production) questions "the place
of criticality in photography writing now". Published and widely
circulated criticality in photography is not diverse or inclusive enough.

Then comes the question of *where* does one find critical thinking
(as opposed to journalism) in photography today? A few online
platforms (in English) exist, a couple of publishers defend it – that's it
(in France, outside academia, it's almost non-existent for example).
Critical consciousness certainly exists, the lack of platforms to
express it is, for me, an important aspect today. Without sounding
boards, it is difficult to develop true debate and exchange or create
space for a diversity of equal voices to express themselves.

Lastly, I feel like the place of criticality in photography writing now
is in complexifying "recently acknowledged" notions/ideas/struggles.
Lately, oppositions around photographer Deana Lawson's iconography
are for me fascinating "places" of criticality, for example. Debate is
probably one of the greatest signs of the recognition of a multi-layered
artist and a complex body of work.

Horacio Fernández

*Horacio Fernández holds a doctorate in Art History
and is an exhibition curator. He has been a university
teacher in the History of Photography for 25 years.
Between 2004–06, he served as the general curator of
PhotoEspaña. He has curated exhibitions such as* Mexicana,
Modern Photography in Mexico *(Institut Valencià d'Art
Modern, Spain, 1998);* Fotografía pública *(Museo Nacional
Centro de Arte Reina Sofía, Madrid and Museo de Bellas
Artes, Bilbao, Spain, 1999);* The Latin American Photobook
(Le Bal, Paris, France, 2012); Photobooks Spain *(Museo
Nacional Centro de Arte Reina Sofía, 2014);* Miserachs
Barcelona *(Museu d'Art Contemporani de Barcelona, Spain,
2015);* New York in Photobooks *(Centro José Guerrero,
Granada, Spain, 2017);* Photobook Phenomenon *(CCCB and
Fundació Foto Colectania, Barcelona);* The Chamber
of Making Poems *(National Library, Madrid, 2018)
and* Photos in Books & Photobooks *(Centro de la Imagen,
México, 2019).*

In 2021, he published Humo/Smoke *(Turner
Publicaciones, 2021), in collaboration with photographer
Adrian Tyler, a photobook that experiments with the
relationship between text and image. His most recent
publication is* Fotografía pública: The Sixties
(CentroCentro, Madrid, 2022). The Latin American
Photobook *(Aperture, 2012) was awarded the best
historical book of the year award at Les Rencontres
d'Arles, France.*

In the early 1990s, I was a university professor writing art criticism. At that time, photography was marginal in the academy, and the art world spoke jargon for the initiated. As a result of my studies in philosophy, I had become an empiricist: photography is necessarily linked to visual reality. So I moved away from art criticism and approached the history of photography. My doctoral thesis on the beauty of technique in the interwar years led me to photographic publications, which were then unexplored territory. The Reina Sofía Museum gave me the opportunity to transform that PhD into *Fotografía Pública*, an exhibition in which there were no photographic prints, something uncommon for the time. Since then, I have worked on a variant of the photographic museum: the library.

Perhaps because intuition is the seed of everything, the first thing to do is to look rather than read. Looking closely at the pictures I am going to write about often helps me not only to ask myself questions, but also to frame the context. I often draw the images to appreciate the details that make them valuable in order to be able to discover the essentials. I also read, of course, but not just theory or photographic criticism. Once the research is finished, it's time to test the ideas and meditate on the authors' intentions and the public's reception.

I usually write about photobooks and their authors. If I can talk to them, I try to do so. If not, I look for their interviews and writings. Photobooks need to work like books: something must happen when turning their pages. Otherwise, we have more than a problem. On the other hand, like almost all books, photobooks are often a team effort. Different contributions are decisive. I am very interested, among other things, in graphic design and in the relationship between text and image.

I am a reader of literature. By this, I mean that reading, whether it is fiction or non-fiction, is not a mere transfer of information for me, but a conversation with an interlocutor who contributes points of view, experiences or doubts. I also appreciate rigorous art history, which considers the artwork as the main document. I look for interpretations and readings that do not intend to be unique or simplifying, as is usually the case in propaganda and politics.

One problem with the history of photography is to believe that all photographs have value. Not everything should be examined, or even preserved. Life is too short to waste time. I am interested in quality and excellence. And also in content, but I believe that content is not obvious in every photograph, because it is 'a secret about a secret', as Diane Arbus said. Exhibitions of photographic publications are still a field of experimentation. In the exhibition, *The Sixties*, that I curated at Centrocentro in Madrid earlier in 2022, there were photobooks, magazines, illustrated books, advertisements, posters and records. That is, a great variety of content and a good list of authors, not only photographers.

What qualities do you admire in other writers?

It is well known that writing something to be remembered means having something to say knowing how to say it and wanting to say it. This requires clarity of language so that expression won't distort thought. And wanting to say something implies having the ability to involve the reader. Once the internet is here, there is no need to demonstrate erudition.

What texts have influenced you the most?

I enjoy the books by Georges Simenon, Bruce Chatwin, W.G. Sebald, J. M. Coetzee or César Aira. I also learn from them, as well as from historians such as Kenneth Clark, Ernst Gombrich, Simon Schama, Orlando Figes, Clément Cheroux or James Elkins. I appreciate the urgent prose of magazines, such as the articles and reviews by Susan Sontag, Teju Cole or Geoff Dyer.

What is the place of criticality in photography writing now?

These are not good times for criticism. If political correctness is added to cancellation, censorship spreads. We need to leave behind the commonplaces of today's Bouvard and Pécuchets and promote heterodox criticism so as to open up new fields and regain the interest of the readers.

Olga Smith

Olga Smith is a historian of contemporary art, writer and curator. As a Marie Skłodowska-Curie Fellow at the University of Vienna, Austria, she is developing a research project with a focus on 'landscape' as a form of picturing nature in the Anthropocene. She writes about photography and new imaging technologies, interchanges between art and intellectual ideas, cultural memory, exhibitions and environmental issues. Her research has been published in French, German and English in journals such as Art History, Moving Image Review & Art Journal *and* Photographies and Fotogeschichte. *She is the author of* Contemporary Photography in France: Between Theory and Practice *(Leuven University Press, 2022), co-editor of* Anamnesia: Private and Public Memory in Modern French Culture *(Peter Lang, 2009) and editor of* Photography and Landscape *(Photographies, 2019).*

Photography was part of my childhood setting in the last decade of the Soviet Union in Tallinn, Estonia. My father could be described as an 'amateur photographer' using Pierre Bourdieu's sociological classification. He spent his free time taking photographs and would periodically set up a darkroom in our functionally cramped Soviet bathroom. It was magical to see images suddenly appear in the chemical bath, although I somehow managed to assist through the entire darkroom process without actually learning how to do it. So photography remained for me a 'theoretical object', to use Rosalind Krauss' words, and eventually the subject of a PhD.

Because I was primarily interested in contemporary art it made sense to do a PhD in art history, although I had no prior training in the discipline. I just wanted to write about artworks, which happened to be made using photography. Although, of course, these seemingly personal choices are determined, to a certain extent, by the context. 10 years ago, when I was staring out on my PhD in the UK, photography was sexy. It was in the museums and galleries, and people were arguing passionately about the consequences of digital convergence, return to materiality, and other questions about what photography is and can be. At the same time, there were very obvious gaps in the history of photography. Available studies systematically under-represented women photographers and offered a very skewed picture of global distribution of photographic practices. Contemporary photography from France was largely missing from these surveys, and from photography discourses. Discovering the writings of Michel Poivert, Dominique Baqué, Régis Durand, François Laruelle and Michelle Debat, amongst others – sadly mostly untranslated into English – I found them refreshingly different, untouched by the ideas of postmodernism or institutional validation that dominated Anglo-American discourses then. These discoveries determined the focus of my PhD.

I was doing my PhD at the University of Cambridge but I was able to spend periods of time in Paris, including through a visiting studentship to the École Normale Supérieure, where I had the wonderful opportunity to meet French scholars, curators and artists. In that period, The Photographers' Gallery in London became an important place for me, as the location for the meetings of Ph: The Photography Research Network, which I co-founded. It was a kind of monthly salon for people writing about photography that provided a much-needed space for exchanges and share opportunities, to give and receive feedback on bits of writing. Most of us were in the various stages of our PhDs that would produce important publications – including Sarah James' *Common Ground* (2013), Martina Caruso's *Italian Humanist Photography* (2016) and Catherine Grant's *Girls! Girls! Girls!* (2011) – and wide-ranging projects such as Annebella Pollen's Mass Observation archive and Sara Knelman's exhibitions. For me, such collective opportunities for exchanges, reflection and critique are indispensable to the process of writing.

The impetus usually comes from an encounter with an artwork, object or text that captivates, vexes, rouses or just makes me want to know more. It can also be a problem, a question that will drive research, which can take years to complete. Throughout this process, I keep notes that feed the writing process, although I sometimes don't follow my own advice to students: keep a reasonably ordered record of your sources and page numbers!

The actual process of writing has changed since the arrival of my children. It is now rigidly scheduled around the available hours of childcare, deadlines, commitments and other constrains. Waiting for the inspiration to strike is not part of this schedule. I set myself a daily target of written words, and it does not matter if all of these words would have to be rewritten the next day, deleted or relegated to a footnote; editing is very much part of writing. What matters is that I have time and space to write, and I have been very fortunate to have had many opportunities for research and writing in my career. Nevertheless, it's a daily struggle, and I often think of Virginia Woolf's words: 'A woman must have money and a room of her own if she is to write fiction.' It's depressing that, a century later, this is still true, and not just for women who want to write fiction.

What are the questions or problems that motivate your writing?

That has changed over the years. When I started writing my PhD, I was interested in photography as a means of perceiving the world, and understanding how artworks, made using the medium of photography, connect with their context – historical, cultural, political and intellectual. This research culminated with the publication of *Contemporary Photography in France* (2022). The book's subtitle, 'between theory and practice', points to the central idea of this book: that in the last 50 years, photography and critical theory in France developed in a state of dialogue. The book traces fascinating interchanges between photographic practices (mostly in art, but also in documentary and fashion) and French theory, in the representative examples of texts by Roland Barthes, Jean Baudrillard and Jacques Rancière.

The question of what it means to write a national history of photography in a globally connected world is still unresolved for me. Evidently, my book on contemporary photography in France was written from a perspective of a foreigner, a non-native speaker of either French or English, which I hope brings a critical distance to the ideas of national identification. Issues of nationality, belonging and immigrant experience feature prominently in the book, and I have also written on these themes with reference to the photography of Mohamed Bourouissa, Bruno Boudjelal and Tobias Zielony. My experience of having been a stateless person, the rise of right-wing nationalism and Brexit have been the factors driving this agenda.

In recent years, the focus of my research has shifted. It expanded beyond the focus on France and photography to focus more broadly the role of global visual culture in shaping a cultural response to climate change. More specifically, my research is directed at analysing the representations of landscapes in contemporary art. My current project, based at the University of Vienna, seeks to understand how new media – including photography – is participating in the evolution of the idea of 'nature' in the age of the Anthropocene. Alongside this project, I am also working with Andrew Patrizio on a collective project with a focus on ecocritical methods: critical frameworks, approaches and practices that will facilitate the work of art historians engaged with the issues of environmental interrelation, sustainability and justice.

These issues are also relevant to current research in photography. What would thinking in terms of planetary, ecological interconnectedness do to existing narratives about national schools of photography? How can we overcome the anthropocentric bias that has hitherto dominated photographic theory? What is the ecological impact of photographic image production? How do we write about images made from materials extracted from Earth?

It depends on the text. I find philosophy and theory difficult; reading it takes a superhuman effort of concentration and it needs time. Reading history, including much of art history, in contract, is more intuitive and straightforward for me as it usually involves narratives, images, concrete examples. My first love, however, is literature, and I do not understand why I have not yet come with a project that would allow me to read prose fiction "for work".

Personally, I am very glad to see that the tendency to use theory to prop up a curatorial concept seems to be on the wane. It used to be the case that you walk into an exhibition and there will be a long, exhausting quote from Gilles Deleuze greeting you. This is not to say that curation, theory and art practices are now completely separate domains. But there seems to me now a more sophisticated and integrated way of bringing them together that I would describe as a co-existing field of practices, defined in terms of overlaps and confrontations rather than linear trajectories of influence.

I admire clarity of ideas and arguments, and the ability to stand back from the views of the others and follow one's own trajectory. I also admire greatly the capacity that some writers have to combine politics and aesthetics in a way that doesn't just use artworks for political engagement, but produces real infight into how they shape our relationship with politics, social relations, environments, and ecologies. I am also really impressed with writing across disciplines that does not exclude those who have not the specific competence for exploring a particular disciplinary territory.

For these reasons, I admire the work of writers such as Jacques Rancière, Abdelmalek Sayad, Kristin Ross, Deborah Willis, Griselda Pollock, Maria Puig de la Bellacasa, Martha Rosler, Geoffrey Batchen, Clément Chéroux, Stuart Hall, Val Plumwood, Sugata Ray, De-nin D. Lee, Oxana Gavrishina, Abigail Solomon-Godeau, Andrew Patrizio, Robin Kelsey, Rebecca Solnit, Ursula K. Heise, David Bate, Mark Cheetham, Vandana Shiva, Gregory Levine, Michel Poivert, Rachael Z. Delue, Lucy R. Lippard, Heather Davis, Kwame Anthony Appiah, Hilde van Gelder… The list is endless and ever-expanding.

Roland Barthes' unique form of subjective writing has always been a fascination for me. What he wrote about photography applies to writing: 'I believe that the photographer is essentially a witness to his own subjectivity, that is to say, the manner in which he presents himself as a subject facing an object.' I find this quality in the writings of Astrida Neimanis, Robin Wall Kimmerer, Rebecca Tamás. And these are just the books currently on my desk, there are many more.

What is the place of criticality in photography writing now?

At a time when climate, national identity and migration present some of the most pressing challenges, criticality is essential to photography writing if it is to remain relevant today.

David Campany

David Campany is a curator, writer and educator. His books include Indeterminacy: thoughts on Time, the Image and Race(ism), *co-authored with Stanley Wolukau-Wanambwa (MACK, 2022);* On Photographs *(Thames & Hudson, 2020);* Walker Evans: The Magazine Work *(Steidl, 2013);* Photography and Cinema *(Reaktion Books, 2008) and* Art and Photography *(Phaidon, 2003). His curatorial projects include* #ICPConcerned: Global Images for Global Crisis *(2020),* The Lives and Loves of Images *(2020) and* A Handful of Dust *(2015).*

'About' is a complicated word. I first started to write during my undergraduate years. I was on a wildly ambitious 50/50 programme, half image-making, half writing, informed by a number of disciplines: semiotics, psychoanalysis, Marxism, feminism, post-colonial theory, theories of institutions and ideology, aesthetics, phenomenology and film theory. Reading preceded any writing. Lots of it. I was struck early on by the difference between writings that began from the particular – this or that image – and writings that began with a theoretical abstraction, and deployed photographs as illustrations or examples. Both have their merit, of course, and I wrote in both ways at that time. Seven or eight years later, opportunities came my way to write for magazines and books, and I had to figure out if I could do something. By then, I had already been teaching for a few years. I suspect the daily practice of getting complex ideas into sentences comprehensible to students shaped how I began to write. As the years passed, I became somewhat averse to writing 'about' photographs, preferring to write around them, off them, in parallel, leaving the image as something for the reader to consider for themself. This came from the realisation of how little words can do in the face of the image, and to pretend otherwise was folly. That 'little' is vitally important, but it *is* little.

What is your writing process?

Everyone has their own creative rhythms and must accept them, because they cannot really be altered. I'm not all that productive but I don't waste time. I usually work on two texts at once because I get stuck so often, and instead of doing nothing I can switch. Most often, I write in order to find out what I think about things, and I try to write in a way that will carry me and the reader through that thinking. That means that the *form* of the writing is always in play, and cannot be taken for granted. I never know if a piece of writing is going to work out.

Occasionally, I've written polemics, and polemical writing was certainly the strongest kind I encountered as a student. I still relish reading strident texts, past and present. They do help to clarify. But I discovered I was temperamentally unsuited to that mode, which is premeditated and programmatic. Writing to discover what you think is quite different. It is speculative, risky, uncharted. Against that, I enjoy the parameter of the word count. If there's no limit, my writing gets baggy. Not always, but often. (Maybe that's why I've never blogged.) Interesting writing can be any length. A hundred words, a thousand, ten thousand.

What opened me up was the realisation that I could include images alongside my words. The richest experiences I'd had as a reader were with writings that included images, mainly in books on cinema. I liked it when the choice and sequence of images threaded through a text seemed almost like a form of writing. My own writing is done this way wherever possible. If I can get the 'image track' to feel interesting, to me at least, I can then begin to write. I don't know of many other writers who do this. My interest in this approach is why I also became a curator and an editor of photographic books. There are parallels. I have often encouraged students to write this way, beginning with the choice of images. I've noticed it can work wonders for smart students who thought they had no chance of writing well, or in a way that they might enjoy and benefit from. If you fear the blank page, put an image on it. (Having the image on the page for the reader to look at for themselves is also a great discipline for a writer.)

I rewrite a lot. Partly, this is because my first drafts are lousy, but I'm trying to get my words to work well on the ear. I'm sure that comes from teaching, but also from the fact that I've always been impressed by good public speaking. If my words are dead to the ear, I know I need to rewrite. That's not a rule for all writing. It just works for me.

The invitation plays a key part. I am fortunate in that institutions, publishers and image-makers often ask me to write. That element of surprise is really useful, as is the feeling of confidence one gets when someone likes your work and thinks you could do something worthwhile. I'm as likely to write for a little-known artist as for a major institution. Follow the work, not the reputation.

Sometimes I would rather not produce a text on my own, feeling I have more interesting things to discuss than to write. In these situations, I'm likely to suggest a conversation or written exchange, rather than an essay. Some of my published conversations – with Jeff Wall, Anastasia Samoylova, Stephen Shore, Sophie Rickett, Stanley Wolukau-Wanambwa and Daniel Blaufuks, for example – are among my favourite writings. I should say here that these conversations really *are* conversations. They are open-ended, speculative, responsive and all about the *exchange* of ideas. I know this project has the word 'Conversations' in its title, but it doesn't really contain conversations. What I'm writing here is a response to a questionnaire: an efficient way to solicit formatted 'content'. That's why the questionnaire is such a dominant form these days. A conversation is the opposite.

Mixed feelings are the best motivation for me as a writer, and as a viewer. If my feelings are too clear to begin with, then there's little in it for me. As for problems, I think the largest one has been the growing gap between writing that takes place in the academy (universities) and writing that takes place outside. I think this is worrying for a society. When I became a writer, having worked in a university for a while, that gap was already becoming very real, and I could see it had political consequences. The smart stuff wasn't getting into the world, and when it did, it was not often understood. As neo-liberal capitalism marched its violent way onwards, the academy retreated from the public square, making its critiques and presenting its alternatives to its peer group, in ways its peer group appreciated. I'm exaggerating, but only slightly. As an emerging writer, I had to face that in a very immediate way. I made the decision, for good or bad, to publish outside of the academy. I've written very few "peer-reviewed" essays for academic journals, for example. (Seriously, who wants to live in a peer-reviewed culture? Sounds vaguely Stalinist to me. Sure, I want my brain surgeon to have read the right journals. Culture is different.) The essays I have written for academic journals were to see if I could do it on those terms, as an exercise. Once I'd ticked that box, I wanted other challenges, other audiences, which I didn't know existed but I had a feeling they might. (I'm always fascinated to see how people who write about photography describe themselves. 'Theorist'. 'Art historian'. 'Critic'. 'Academic'. The aversion to the term 'Writer' says a lot.)

There is such anxiety around images. Rightly so, and for a lot of reasons. But there is a tendency for writing, for writers on the visual arts, to step in and overwrite, to attempt to supply the 'script for looking', to take away the anxiety the image produces and stabilise things. More often than not, this is prejudice and preference masquerading as reason. One sees this in everything from museum wall texts, to reviews, blogs and critiques. Images get "explained" in terms of authorial intention, biography, strategy, what we "ought" to be thinking, and so forth. This runs the risk of diminishing us all as viewers, patronising us while pretending to enlighten. Moreover, it refuses the essential ambiguity of images. There are forms of writing that don't do this, that keep the door open, however awkward and painful that can be. Ambiguity, the openness of the image, can be an anxious problem… But it is the only way out, so we ought to embrace it.

The other problems that motivate my writing are self-imposed. They involve finding new relations between image, thought and language.

Pretty voracious and wide-ranging. I am also a re-reader. Texts can be returned to, in order to figure out how they were written, and as a way of measuring one's own intellectual and emotional development. There are novels and philosophical essays I make an effort to reread every few years. They stay the same. I change.

I had no idea curation was so prominent. Nevertheless, writing is writing and curation is curation. They share some concerns and approaches, of course, but, as a writer and a curator, I'm interested in the differences.

Unimprovable sentences. The ability to get paid. (As far as I know, we're all doing this project for nothing.)

Influence is largely unconscious, so don't ask *me*. I am not being flippant. The answers we give about our influences are merely the answers we are able to give. Among my conscious answers, the ones that come readily to mind are the writings of Roland Barthes (on almost anything other than photography), Susan Sontag (same), Jacques Derrida, Fred Moten, Susan Stewart, Fredric Jameson, Raul Ruiz, Clarice Lispector, Marguerite Duras, Julia Kristeva, Gilles

Deleuze, Victor Burgin, Frantz Fanon, Adam Phillips, George Orwell, Lydia Davis, Samuel Beckett and Virginia Woolf. I would give a different answer tomorrow, I'm sure. Between what we know and what we don't, there are hunches and intuitions. I have a hunch that the texts influencing me most profoundly were, and are, song lyrics. Words *as sung.* I cannot memorise a line of poetry, even if it means the world to me. I remember songs without even trying. I cannot imagine this has not had an effect, but I am not sure I could define it.

There are many places. It's good to be mindful of this.

The space of critical refusal interests me. For example, how would discussions about *identity* take shape if one considered the possibility that the most interesting and profound things about identity do not offer themselves to the camera, to visibility? Or, what do we do about the fact that the narrowly consensual categories of both the mass media and art world demand certain conformities? At what points and in what situations might a commitment to photography be a walking away from it, and a turning towards something else, either as a maker, writer or viewer? There are photographers who face these questions and find other ways. And there are writers who have advocated for this too. The endless 'commitment' to photography, the presumption that all things of value can and must be available to its often-crushing and limiting embrace, is a very real issue. This should be faced as a matter of some urgency. (I don't feel committed to photography at all *costs*, merely fascinated by it, and life beyond it is rich.) Critical refusal ought to be a vital part of the way photography is thought, discussed, taught and written. It should always be on the table. There are many positive signs that this is happening.

Daniel C. Blight

Daniel C. Blight is a writer based in London and Lecturer in Photography (Historical & Critical Studies) at University of Brighton. Recent work includes "Ways of Seeing Whiteness" in George Yancy: A Critical Introduction, *eds. Kimberley Ducey, Joe R. Feagin and Clevis Headley (Rowman & Littlefield, 2021) and* The Image of Whiteness: Contemporary Photography and Racialization *(SPBH Editions/ Art on the Underground, 2019). He is currently working on a monograph,* Photography's White Racial Frame *(Bloomsbury, 2024), and slowly completing a PhD in the faculty of Social Science and Public Policy at King's College London. In 2022, he served as Visiting Scholar, Department of Art and Art History, University of Utah, Salt Lake City.*

I developed an interest in photography via post-rock and "electronica" album covers. The cityscape on the front of Fugazi's *End Hits* (1998), the obliquely angled road sign on Hoover's *The Lurid Traversal of Route 7* (1994), or the pixelated "terrain" on the cover of Autechre's *Incunabula* (1993) LP, which I took to be extra-terrestrial Swindon as I walked its streets, mashed at night, strangely under-stimulated. 20 years ago in that place, I made digital photographs and electronic music as part of a photography foundation course at Swindon College because, having quit my A Levels to become a pizza chef, it was the only route to university, an overdraft and a student loan.

My work then involved software editing digital photographs into CD artwork for the glitchy music I was making. I recorded the mechanical sounds of analogue camera shutters, cutting them up and sequencing them into drumbeats, and then manipulating tonally-inverted photographs of lightning to visually represent the glitches. It was as bad as it sounds. One of the compositions I completed then was titled *Just take the fucking photo*. This was the first time I wrote about photographs – or should that be "photography"? – eventually repeating the phrase into a microphone and layering the recorded voice track over camera shutter rhythms constructed in Fruity Loops, an audio sequencer of sorts.

My first experience of writing about photography is a species of repetitive song lyric: "Just take the fucking photo", I wrote aggressively, over and over, on a piece of note paper in my teenage bedroom. In a sense, all my writing about photography since then has been born from the frustration captured in that phrase. Although I like to think I'm able to work with more "complex" forms of writing nowadays, there is a large part of me that appreciates teenage quotidian writing, an adolescent poetic writing, a writing apart from the perceived maturity of scholarly aptitude and normative citation practices.

On reflection, I feel there is something to learn from my frustration. What if my writing *is* frustration? What if I was supposed to be a writer not because I had anything interesting to say, but so that I could enjoy all the other things I do because my frustrations were absorbed by and confined to my writing? I count myself lucky that I have figured out how to confine frustration. I've sealed it into a sort of literary defeat.

'Process' sounds like such a clinical and serious word to describe how I write, although I like the sound of one of the word's synonyms – 'unfolding'. A procrastinatory unfolding. I enjoy reducing myself to a state of under-stimulation over a period of two or three days. Eventually, boredom compels me to write. At that point the smallest thing feels new, wakes me up and gets me excited again. Often cooking, or fixating on a particular image in a book.

I spend most of my time not writing. I find this a necessary part of the process leading up to the act itself (which is both a struggle and a performance to myself – can I do it? Should I do it? Will it work?). Things don't unfold this way deliberately. Most of the time, I just can't write. It seems too hard, too difficult. I think coming to terms with this is the most important part of my writing in a philosophical sense. I like the idea, more and more, of slow writing, and of selective writing.

The rest is practical: reading, mostly on a screen, apart from poetry which I tend to read on paper. Looking at pictures in printed books. Making mental notes. Forgetting things. Then eventually I write something when I feel I can. I collect quotations when I'm reading. When I'm writing essays, I often use these to structure text. I write before them, after them, in the middle of them to disrupt them, and to see what happens. I largely write in incoherent, broken fragments which I call paragraphs. I can't always be clear because I don't really know what I mean. I call this writerly honesty. I'm trying to describe a feeling using words that are always wrong.

Since 2013, I've been making visual cues to aid my writing. I call these *Image Reconstructions* and they are collages comprised of visual symbols that summarise the subjects of texts I am working on. I collect images in folders as I research and read: the QAnon "logo", a photograph of some weed, a Creative Commons image of oil burning on the surface of the sea, a .png of a pizza held up by a white hand. I then group them together into meaningful compositions (see the image *nug*, 2021). The rest is a weird form of visualisation in which images come to life through speculation, appropriation, trying things out to visually represent meaning. Sometimes I can't finish the essay, or the poem, and it instead becomes an image reconstructed from the practice of writing. Sometimes I can't finish the image. Most of the time nothing is finished, and nothing gets made, and that's OK too.

It sounds a cliché – and I hate the empty verbosity of the conceptual framing – but I prefer to write *with* photographs rather than *about* or, in the oft-repeated phrase, *on* them. I produce an essay plan using images and quotations in close and strange juxtapositions. I look for resonances, contradictions, parallels. My habits have been reformed by The Virus and by family life, particularly children. I no longer feel a need to write all the time. Most of the time I just don't want to. I'd rather read or listen. I write towards happiness and in the direction of freedom. I'm much more comfortable with that cliché.

In a sense, this isn't true because I write many more short poems than I do long essays. Perhaps a poem a month, and two or three essays a year? I politely decline most invitations to write short form for magazines and newspapers nowadays. There are other people much better placed to comment on new projects and exhibitions than I am. There are certain spaces I don't wish to occupy any longer. I am also disillusioned with the way badly paid short form essay writing for magazines and newspapers forces me to focus on some specious idea of *right now*, responding to "current practice". Slow writing is something that the world of photography magazines can't contend with, but they need it badly. Slow writing is a needed practice in academia too, in which scholars are forced to produce at pace to satisfy the various "excellence frameworks" they are compelled to adhere to. How many journal articles do I need to get a promotion? Are we talking 10 mediocre articles, or one bad boy one? Who gets to decide whether I'm any good or not?

If "right now" is both a fashionable position culturally speaking, and a global catastrophe unfolding in strikingly visual terms (images of the sea on fire, shamanic QAnon fascists storming the Capitol, Boris Johnson talking shit on the BBC), I'm looking to respond more slowly certainly. Part of what capitalism's recently rejuvenated intersection with fascism requires of us is that we keep up. Move fast and stay relevant! I'm not the first person to say we should refuse that. I want to go back to a time when I could walk the streets stoned at night *slowly* with nowhere to be. I want to make pizzas for minimum wage again. But this time they're texts, and I get to bake them for longer than four minutes. Unfortunately weed makes me puke now, so I can't smoke, and I earned more money working as a waiter at Pizza Express than I do as an academic.

Slow writing is a form of epistemic protest. It says to me: stop producing knowledge habitually until you understand your own epistemic standpoint. Or: work to produce a kind of counter-knowledge that supports other people. Slowing down is me trying to be less selfish. Perhaps the "knowledge" I possess is a form of what Charles W. Mills called 'white ignorance' before he recently passed. I have thought about this in more detail in a chapter for a new book on the philosopher George Yancy. In that essay, I consider his work, his excellence, and myself, *as I am*.

What are the questions or problems that motivate your writing?

I write to edge away from the disappointment of my social self. To be white, and to be a man, is in two interlinked ways to be a problem. Therefore, the superficial problem of my work is me, and by extension the fundamental problems are white supremacy and the elite white male dominance system. I write in the hope that I can become someone else, someone better. I am in my own way, tripping over my own feet. This is a process of discovery in which my social self is cracked open; breached to form a sort of aperture. I want to write despite myself. I have come to understand this more recently as a willingness on my part to become vulnerable, to fail publicly, to not care about the consequences of doing so. It's only through a kind of risk that anything meaningful can come of my writing. The trouble is risk is predominantly about failure. My process is just that, then: attempt to escape myself; fail. A strangely productive failure.

Isn't it true that writers can't name themselves? My writing began with frustration, and its continuation now involves wondering whether what I write next will result in another "race traitor!" death threat via email. Yet, with this violence in mind, how can I not name myself? I am a white writer coming to terms with what it's like to unravel in words. I think all white writers should try this. This is not a melancholy unfolding though, and it is not one that requires any emotional sympathy, nor undue attention. I am deeply happy. I am filled with love for other people's writing, other people's poetry, other people – for the first time in a long time.

What kind of reader are you?

I read long essays quickly and short poems slowly. Then I read the same essays slowly and have no time left to read poems. I read with admiration, curiosity, frustration. I read searching for something I never find.

What do you go looking for in your reading?

I look for a mix of deep exegesis and personal reflection. Often one leads to the other. It's sort of like asking what I go looking for in food. How much time do I have? Am I in the mood to cook? Do I have a Tesco lasagne I can put in the microwave, squirt extra ketchup on top of, and dip chunks of garlic bread into? Or am I in a Michelin Star pub for my birthday rinsing it hard on my credit card? When I read, I gorge uncertainly, and its often done in such a way that makes me feel I'm avoiding rather than looking for things. I'm avoiding writers like me. I do think "What do I want to read?" before I read sometimes, but it's not like I always have much choice when one article takes me via a hyperlink to another, over and over again. I've read so much, partially. I keep trying to read in print again, and then I start missing all the hyperlinks, the distractions on Wikipedia, the stopping and searching for things I don't understand in journal articles on the University of Brighton's online library.

I enjoy reading my student's essays. They teach me how to read and they teach me how to write. It's a wonderful thing, teaching. I used to conceptualise it as something I did to feed myself so I could concentrate on my writing, but now it's a thing I do to actively learn. I read with pleasure in a community of student-scholars. This year, I will work with students to encounter racial whiteness in reading photographs. This is a process in which we "let go" of the white logic and white racist visual foundations that underpin the western colonial history of photography and instead turn our attention to forms of white uncertainty. Irrespective of our individual racial identifications, we all work together in a white university. In a white space. In white complicity pedagogy, this involves de-centring forms of "knowing" and instead centres notions of white humility ("I do not know"/"I am not sure") and white listening – learning to listen while giving up on needing to feel like a "good" white scholar. I take my lead here from educators such as Barbara Applebaum, Stephen Brookefield and Zeus Leonardo.

Reading should always be paired with writing. This doesn't necessarily mean essay writing, but perhaps a simpler form of writing notes, questions or incomplete fragments. I encourage students to read in such a way that *excites* them to produce fragments of text, as roughly as they like. We then work through those texts together and make sense of them in critical relation to scholarly conventions. What results is a form of photo-textual essay practice; a manner of *writing with* photographs in order to produce literary essays that respond both to a history of the essay form in photographic cultures, and importantly, embodied, reflexive and phenomenological approaches to images derived from methods in visual sociology. It sounds technical, but it's exciting, in practice, in the classroom.

The sort of canonical history of photography taught in British Higher Education is undergirded by the white logic of European settler colonialism. This isn't discussed nearly enough, and it has a huge impact on what is often falsely named *the* history of photography and how we theorise its structures and meanings (in this way history and theory go hand in hand). We desperately need new historical and theoretical frameworks because the European invention of photography from the 1830s – which is not the first invention of photography, but rather the most convenient white inauguration – is founded upon the same intellectual traditions that justify the genocide of Indigenous, Black and Brown people the world over. After Gerald Horne, let's call this tradition the apocalypse of settler colonialism, and, after Charles W. Mills, let's call it the white ignorance of epistemological individualism in the historical project of racial liberalism. In short, white supremacy continues to govern the world at large, and all cultural phenomena including photography falls within its scope and power.

More precisely, the European invention of photography, which is to say the "fixing" of images by such figures as William Henry Fox Talbot in the middle of the 19th century (some 200 years after the invention of racial whiteness), is a visual project that inherits the social dynamics of what Joe R. Feagin calls the white racial frame and extends this into particular types of "image-schema". This image-schema, which I am theorising in a new book, *Photography's White Racial Frame*, can be described in several ways. It is first and foremost a mental frame, or what has been described differently as the colonial gaze by Frantz Fanon and Edward Said. More precisely, this mental frame is named white scopophilia by George Yancy, and a regime of seeing by Kalpana Seshadri-Crooks. These concepts share a common truth: that with the invention of racial whiteness came what might be called a psychology of colonial picturing. This is a form of white imaginary, which is of course etymologically to say *white imagery*. We white people look at the world through what Stuart Hall called a white eye, and we do so full of an often-unconscious desire for power, wealth and knowledge. Photography is the great inheritor of this perceptual frame, this image-schema and its false narrative of white violence *then* and white innocence *now*. Thus, I theorise the European history of photography as a white racist visual dynamic full of emancipatory potential in the hands of those artists that choose to work against it. Like racial whiteness, photography can be abolished.

Understanding the significant violence of this visual framework should result in nothing less than seeing the world in an entirely new way, and as I have contended, seeing one's white self in an entirely new way. If curation is the care and organisation of cultural phenomena, then in a white supremacist world it either stands within or without the white racial frame. The practice of curating is a historical and theoretical positioning which takes place in relation to the history of the western museum defined as (what Dan Hicks calls) 'white infrastructure'. So, the question becomes, why is curating now so prominent? And for me, the answer has to do with the false choices racial whiteness continues to offer curators (remember, everyone is a curator, but it is most often white people that declare themselves so or who are awarded the title institutionally). To curate is first to possess knowledge, and then to make choices based on that knowledge resulting in some objects getting attention and others not. Possession is privilege. Knowledge is racialised, gendered, made bodily. Which curatorial bodies are most prominent? Ones like mine. Like racial whiteness, white curators can be abolished too.

Your book The Image of Whiteness, *examining photography's construction and perpetuation of racialised hierarchy,*

     Daniel C. Blight

The Image of Whiteness is visually intrusive and conceptually shocking for lots of white people – certainly if encountered as an exhibition, in a public museum space (white infrastructure). I owe this to the artists featured. They have done the work and I have brought it together. I think it would be interesting if there was an accompanying events programme in which people could thrash out some of the ideas in the project. George Yancy might deliver the keynote on the question of symbolic white death – he's an excellent public speaker – and I could be available as white visitors feel more and more uncomfortable, just like I do every day as I try to learn about my white self. I would be there to care for them (the curator's role), not to make them feel good but to make them understand that it's OK to feel uncomfortable and confused by something we are only just coming to understand: that being white is to embody a violent lie; that the exhibition is teaching us that we have been lied to, and that we are upholding that lie and that what we need do is *look*, and then *see* differently, and *listen* attentively. That's what I hope *The Image of Whiteness* is about: rendering white people uncomfortable so that we can be challenged and then learn. We white people need to learn to *feel* – to racially empathise – and then to self-disclose. I'm not interested in books or exhibitions that revive whiteness or make it "good". That is an impossibility. A paradoxical space of both white projection and display.

White self-disclosure starts from the position that there is 'no contradiction in whites working as anti-racists and their being racist,' as Stephen Brookefield writes. So, I start from that position in my own work, and when I encounter white denialists – those individuals socialised white that have unfortunately still not realised their racial whiteness has very little to do with their skin colour – I seek to help them through a form of creative care. Imagine if that could be communicated to an exhibition audience? This is not to say white viewers should be told they are racist upon entry to the museum, but that they will surely come to realise to be white is to be racist by the time they leave. The exhibition becomes a form of white abolitionist narrative disclosure in which white people are prompted to learn through a process of looking and seeing differently.

Whatever *The Image of Whiteness* is, I hope it is not a mere anti-racist declaration. I am interested in avoiding spaces of epistemic comfort for myself and other white people. I want to create thankful spaces in which abolitionist practice is uncomfortable and ongoing. An anti-white social ontology requires a complex theory of practice that understands the space between white agency and white social structure as a fissure in which a series of epistemic possibilities might be revealed. My writing, and any exhibition making that follows it, is about *revealing* in this way. I reject error avoidance as I will make errors as I go. In a sense to be white is to be a human error, so what would it be like to accept that glitch in the social matrix from the get-go? What if instead of conceptualising my work as "good" I call it an error – which is different from a mistake – and brings me all the way back to where I started: frustration, erratum, not writing until I have something to say, or rather, something *to do*.

What qualities do you admire in other writers?

I admire anyone who has the courage to write against themselves.

What texts have influenced you the most?

Here's what is influencing me this week: *Simple Men* (2019) by Rachael Allen; *To Revive a Person is No Slight Thing* (2016) by Diane Williams; *White Self-Criticality Beyond Anti-Racism: How Does it Feel to Be a White Problem?* (2014), edited by George Yancy; *Weird Fucks* (1980) by Lynne Tillman; *Black Bodies, White Gold* (2021) by Anna Arabindan-Kesson.

What is the place of criticality in photography writing now?

Criticism gets me in trouble. Always with white people in positions of power, which is reason enough to keep getting in trouble.

Zoé Samudzi

*Zoé Samudzi is an Assistant Professor in Photography
at the Rhode Island School of Design, Providence, US,
a Research Associate at the Center for the Study of
Race, Gender and Class at the University of Johannesburg,
South Africa, and a member of the Race, Medicine and
Social Justice research cluster at the Center for
the Study of Slavery and Justice at Brown University,
Providence. She is also an Associate Editor at*
Parapraxis Magazine, *and her writing has appeared
in* Artforum, The New Republic, Art in America,
The New Inquiry, The Architectural Review, *SFMOMA's*
Open Space *and elsewhere.*

I started writing about photographs around the same time I started trying to take them. I got a second-hand camera in the summer of 2017 because I wanted to learn how to do something new: I wanted to nurture a skill I didn't have because my years of focusing single-mindedly on my academic work had left me risk-averse (afraid to try things I wouldn't immediately be good at), incurious and without hobbies. I took some pictures I loved (and more that I didn't) and I had an artist residency with the Ashara Ekundayo Gallery in Oakland in 2018 where I exhibited some photographs I took back home in Zimbabwe. But I quickly realised that I loved reading and writing about photography more than I enjoyed creating images, and I started focusing more on the monographs and theory I'd purchased – the problematic favourite David Goldblatt, Santu Mofokeng, Susan Sontag, Roland Barthes, John Berger, Okwui Enwezor, Roy DeCarava and Langston Hughes' *Sweet Flypaper of Life* (1955), Samuel Fosso, Carrie Mae Weems, Malick Sidibé and a bunch of others. The short time I spent as a member of the Black Aesthetic, a Bay Area collective focused on Black visual culture, is really what animated my writing. I had the privilege of editing a collection of writing with the collective around the same, and I had a column with the now defunct *New Life Quarterly* where I had the opportunity to begin synthesising infant thoughts about violence and the image. I was also a docent at Pier 24 Photography in the fall of 2019, so I got to spend every Monday drinking in the details of the 10-year retrospective "Looking Back" and interacting with museumgoers; I spent my downtime scribbling away in my notebook (I always carry a notebook or loose paper), so I consider these months as a part of this formative writing time as well.

I started writing about photographs more seriously in the last two years of my PhD (2019–21). My doctoral work was about the Ovaherero and Nama genocide and the entanglements of bioscience and biomedicine in imperial German racecraft: reading and writing about the ethnographic photographs taken by German anthropologists lent itself to broader considerations of racialised people and their bodies across space and time. Writing about contemporary photography as a critic strengthened my sociological analysis, and I feel grateful that I can bring those writerly sensibilities together in the classes I teach about photography.

I do a lot of writing by hand, which forces me to slow down and encourages me to think more expansively.

My first step is to draw a map linking together the concepts I (think I) want to address. In the next iteration, I arrange the non-linear web of ideas into an argument and signpost citations or related work by others. By the time I sit down in front of my computer, the majority of the conceptual heavy lifting is finished and I'm just focusing on the piece's connective tissue. I've been writing like this for eight or nine years now. I've found it helps to reduce the amount of time spent sitting in front of a demoralisingly empty Word document *and* there's often an excess of material that ends up getting absorbed into other work.

I love and need routines, and at my most diligent, I like to wake up and do unprompted and directionless writing first thing in the morning: a dump of fragmented thoughts unmediated by a social media-shortened attention span. After a couple years of doing this, I've come to realise that I write the same things over and over until they're either refined enough for an outside reader or sufficiently clarified for myself. I think an embrace of reiteration is my writing ethos in this moment where I'm trying to figure out what and where my political and critical priorities lie.

What are the questions or problems that motivate your writing?

Violence. I'm consumed by racial capitalism's production of the transnational matrix of cannibalistic and suicidal violence and how that violence is normalised or justified or internalised through the visual's structuring of difference. I have a beat-up copy of Arundhati Roy's *The Algebra of Infinite Justice* (2001) that I bought back in 2011 when I spent the summer after my freshman year working at a training hospital in Medchal, about 25-miles away from Hyderabad in the former state of Andhra Pradesh – now Telangana – in south-eastern India. I didn't realise that I'd arrived in the midst of an ongoing (and occasionally violent) secession struggle: there was a mass resignation of Telangana ministers from the Andhra Pradesh Assembly that July, there was a bandh (a shutdown) and I watched Telegu-language coverage of people burning effigies of the ministers that didn't resign. I don't understand Telugu, so all I had were English-speaking citizen journalists and commentators on Twitter, an occasional interpretation of events from a co-worker or resident in the women's hostel where I was staying, the images I saw on television and Roy's synthesis of caste and classed inequality in India.

In the book's titular chapter, Roy describes the Western imperialist calculus of human life that has become central in my own considerations of how structural violences preclude autonomy, safety and self-fashioning for their targets: what Frantz Fanon describes as the ontological flaw of colonised people (particularly Black people) and their existence through a racial imaginary of domination. She writes:

> *'So here we have it. The equivocating distinction between civilisation and savagery, between the "massacre of innocent people" or, if you like, "a clash of civilisations" and "collateral damage." The sophistry and fastidious algebra of Infinite Justice. How many dead Iraqis will it take to make the world a better place? How many dead Afghans for every dead American? How many dead children for every dead man? How many mujahideen for each dead investment banker?'*

I was 16 in January 2009 when George W. Bush left office and Barack Obama was inaugurated: I was two months shy of my ninth birthday when I came home from school and my father told me that bad people had crashed airplanes into the World Trade Center on 11 September 2001. I came into political maturity watching the invasion of Afghanistan and then Iraq, Israeli children drawing smiley faces on the rockets that would be dropped in Lebanon during Israel's 2006 war with Hezbollah, and the incommensurable horror of the torture and humiliation in Abu Ghraib. While there were massive anti-war protests during the Bush administration, I now realise how many of these images were intended to manufacture consent: the videos of madrasas (alleged terrorist training camps) and angry protestors (said terrorists) burning the stars and stripes and chanting "Death to America!" were evidence of Arab/Muslim evil in the Middle East that justified the US government's campaign to snuff it out by any means necessary. I cried a lot to my father when we'd watch the news because the unfairness of war seemed much more straightforward and obvious to me than it was to politicians that lied to the United Nations about the existence of weapons of mass destruction: it's not really a surprise to me that I study genocide now.

Kimberly Juanita Brown's "Regarding the Pain of the Other: Photography, Famine, and the Transference of Affect" (2014) – an essay I return to constantly and feel privileged to finally be able teach – is a rebuttal to the humanist thesis at the heart of Sontag's *Regarding the Pain of Others* (2003). Brown ultimately concludes that images of the suffering of "others" animate a perverse reassurance and reify the affective chasm between "us" and "them." I'm preoccupied with understanding and figuring out which fact pattern – to borrow from a friend who was describing the sequence of texts people consume that ultimately justify Palestinian suffering – can sufficiently disrupt normative white supremacist structures and scripts materialised in the image. This mission feels increasingly urgent as we're inundated with photographs of rapidly accelerating ecological collapse that is overwhelmingly impacting regions of the world that are both not responsible for environmental destruction and have been rendered as the conquerable zone of non-being.

Maybe this is a naive oversimplification, but I guess I just really need to understand why we're so comfortable watching people die.

It seems especially striking, thinking through Brown, that our shorthands for what we think images do are quite far from their effects or consequences: we describe images as revealing or exposing, when in many cases they conventionalise or, as you say, comfort. Do you think language can play a role in this? Is there is a different possible way for discussing, and therefore thinking, imagery in order to get close to violence and its perpetuity?

I think an affective overhaul is in order, particularly in our understanding of empathy as a collective political emotion. On one hand, we're allegedly able to know, understand and commemorate the victims of violence by visualising and committing to memory the harms and atrocities to which they're subjected. But as abject violence must occur again and again, what does it mean to watch it happen again and again? Is the act of witnessing an act of empathy? And what does it mean that images of atrocity win international awards for photography or journalism even as the conflicts rage on? Is our common humanity really heightened when we witness other people's suffering? Do repeated encounters with the ubiquity of excess suffering nurture a kind of nihilism about the inevitability of suffering, or do these visual endeavours in truth-telling meet the same fate as fine art photography? I don't think empathy is the imagination of your own experience of some situation or the creation of analogy to make another's suffering more legible: this compounded with a sympathetic display of the piteous situation of some other seems to animate the circulation of images of conflict. You cannot pass off a selfish attempt at replicating and exteriorising your own interiority as empathy, because one's moral world has to be completely transformed in order to truly understand another's experience in its own right. I think often about what Édouard Glissant wrote about the right to opacity: 'It is not necessary to try to become the other (to become other) nor to "make" him in my image. These projects of transmutation […] have resulted from the worst pretensions and the greatest magnanimities on the part of the West.'

The production of empathy as we know it, I think, is actually just about legibility: the assimilation of others into a framework of sameness and similarity. That is the antithesis of solidarity or anything that animates a useful response beyond a self-placating sense of guilt. With this reorientation, I think we might have to similarly reappraise photojournalism.

Maybe this isn't a great habit, but I tend to, when I can, read the bibliography first. I like to know ahead of time how and where a writer situates their work: the genealogies into which they place themselves, their citational politics and ethics (or lack thereof). I really appreciate writers who aren't reserved in their use of footnotes. I loved Katherine McKittrick's *Dear Science and Other Stories* (2020) because of her refusal to marginalise her marginalia. Footnotes are where some of her/the best magic happens: where "tangents" are actually offerings of new and familiar conceptual connections, as well as insights into a writer's arrangement of thoughts and their inner monologue.

My attention span hasn't completely returned since I finished my dissertation last year, so I'm still reading economically like a graduate student. I tend to know what I'm interested in for a particular project and focus on that, but if I'm building from scratch (like with the manuscript I've restructured again and again), I read as much and as widely as I'm able. And also, to contradict myself, I have a small pantheon of foundational texts that serve as my North Stars: a dear friend of mine has a running joke that I'm banned from referencing these people in conversation, I'm that serious about keeping them in constant circulation. There are just some texts you read and hold dear (including Berger's 2007 *Hold Everything Dear*) because they teach you how to become the writer you want to be – I try to read these, even in pieces, as often as possible.

Incredibly significant, especially because people and institutions sometimes seem to believe that (curatorial or artistic) intention can supersede centuries of racial semiotics that materialise in and through the photograph or that marginalised identity alone is carte blanche for making thoughtful art.

Absolutely the former. I'm unconvinced that the structures are invisible, even and especially to people in power. They're out in the open! There's a way that the desire for representation really reads as a desire to be known: for a recognition that engenders full citizenship, i.e. assimilability into humanness. It feels like, for many, the redress of genuine historical grievance is increased proximity to the structures of power and capital rather than a destruction of the system altogether – that the resolution for the overdetermination of the nature and content of minoritised people's art and the people themselves is for the same systems to acknowledge and affirm our value and the value of our work. But beyond deciding that insurgent work has *market* value (which is what I think the narrative of the "renaissance of Black art" at the end of the 2010s was mostly about), I'm not sure that's possible. I'm not sure that art institutionality can exist beyond a world that can only exist because of Black death, carcerality, ableism, transantagonism, settler colonialism and all the rest.

I'm not quite as cynical as Mark Fisher because I do believe in the potential of abolitionist and anti-colonial worldmaking and I'm unconvinced by Francis Fukuyama's claim that the end of history is liberal democracy. But I am compelled by Fisher's statement that 'the power of capitalist realism derives in part from the way that capitalism subsumes and consumes all of previous history.' We've seen the agility of art institutions in absorbing and redeploying in their favour existentially damning critique. A lot of work concerned with representation fails to contend with that, or perhaps more worrisomely, isn't concerned with it at all.

Patience, diligence and thoroughness. I am an impatient writer, and I love encountering writers that you can tell have been poring over their subject matter. Patience is poetic, and the writing feels infused with a rhythm of deliberateness that's magnetic. I admire a courageous writer: someone whose writing reflects a set of stakes and urgencies, vulnerable writing that has a lot to lose. I'm always excited by curiosity, and by a writer that's honest about ambivalences and contradictions.

Silencing the Past (1995) by Michel-Rolph Trouillot, *Ways of Seeing* (1972), *A Seventh Man* (1975) and the "Revolutionary Undoing" chapter in *Landscapes* (2016) by Berger, *The Body in Pain* (1985) by Elaine Scarry, *Chromophobia* (2000) by David Batchelor, Sontag's essay "Fascinating Fascism" (1974), *Playing in the Dark* (1992) by Toni Morrison, *The Racial Contract* (1997) by Charles Mills, *Ghostly Matters* (1997) by Avery Gordon and *Black Skin, White Masks* (1952) by Fanon have all been foundational in different ways. I constantly reread Roland Barthes' *A Lovers Discourse* (1977): there's a utility in the romantic lexicon he offers, as well as the one Milan Kundera lends readers in *The Unbearable Lightness of Being* (1984).

More than specific texts, there are authorly and scholarly and mentorly influences. Non-exhaustively and in no order: Tina M. Campt, Christina Sharpe, Saidiya Hartman, Nicholas Mirzoeff, Susan Meiselas,

Charmaine Nelson, Ariella Aïsha Azoulay, Edward Said, Steve Biko, Aimé Césaire, Simone Weil, Allan Sekula, William Blake, Sarah Kane, B.R. Ambedkar and Bertolt Brecht.

There are also concepts that have really stuck with me and shaped how I approach big questions like Michelle Wright's 'epiphenomal time', Gilles Deleuze and Félix Guattari's rhizome, Didier Bigo's 'banopticon', Achille Mbembe's necropolitics, Paul Virilio on picnolepsy, Helga Tawil-Souri's 'checkpoint time', Walter Benjamin's 'aestheticisation of politics', Terence Ranger's 'patriotic history' and so many others.

Instead of this over-emphasis on offering new grammars of interpretation and meaning-making, I think criticality should offer reflections on how to assimilate the things we view and the feelings that arise upon viewing into our everyday lives – a move to begin engaging and resolving that sense of arrest and despairing engulfment that Berger describes in "Photographs of Agony" (1972). Novelty is nice, but a deep engagement of the quotidian and the taken-for-granted, especially when the quotidian is (existential) violence, is even better.

I've only just begun teaching, but I've found that offering my students more questions than "answers" has produced some really thoughtful discussion. I try to encourage an embrace of multiplicity – resolution that resides in a constellation of ideas and a confidence in having their own truth(s) challenged or embracing a multiplicity of truths even as it might be unsettling (and sometimes it should be!). I'm not interested in telling them what or how to think: I think my job as an instructor is just to offer tools to encourage expansive consideration and trust that they know what to do.

Christopher Pinney

Christopher Pinney is Professor of Anthropology and Visual Culture at University College London. He has held visiting positions at the Australian National University, Canberra, University of Chicago, US, University of Cape Town, South Africa, Northwestern University, Evanston, Illinois, US, Boğaziçi University, Istanbul, Turkey, and Jagiellonian University, Krakow, Poland. In 2019, he was a Visiting Professor at EHESS, Paris, France, and delivered a series of GIAN lectures at Jawaharlal Nehru University, Delhi, India.

His research interests cover the art and visual culture of South Asia, with a particular focus on the history of photography and chromolithography in India. He has also worked on industrial labour and Dalit goddess possession. Amongst his publications are Camera Indica (1997), Photos of the Gods (2004), The Coming of Photography in India (2008), Photography and Anthropology (2011), The Waterless Sea (2018) and Lessons from Hell (2018). He is currently leading the ERC Advanced Grant project Citizens of Photography: The Camera and the Political Imagination.

I first got interested in photography during my PhD fieldwork in central India in the early 1980s and I wrote about it in my fieldnotes. I was living in a village and my neighbours kept bringing photographs (and the process of being photographed) to my attention. However, I still had a thesis to write about industrial workers (in central India) so it took me several more years to focus on photography in any kind of writing destined for an audience. I should also declare that other kinds of "photos" (the term used in much of India to also describe chromolithographs) have always interested me as much as the camera-produced variety.

What is your writing process?

Generally chaotic and exploiting the just-in-time principle to the limit. My workspaces rapidly start to look like W.C. Fields' desk in *Man on a Flying Trapeze* (1935) (stratigraphised with ancient papers). This is one of the reasons I've always enjoyed visiting professorships: you usually get an empty office and a clean slate. I still have fond memories of a month in 2000 spent in the History Department at University of Cape Town in an empty office decked with endless shelving on which I could spread my papers.

What are the questions or problems that motivate your writing?

I have no interest in questions that foreground intention, artistry and aura. I'm engaged with the political potentials of "demotic" (aka "vernacular") images, medium specificity and the return of the archaic in the modern. More specifically, the 'exorbitance' and contingency of images, and photographers (as Walter Benjamin proposed) as the 'descendants of the augurs and haruspices'. I see these as all connected: exorbitance is a reflection of medium specificity and explains the excessive information that fills photographs with divinatory potential. I'm currently thinking about the "demotic" as a "more than local, less than global" alternative to the "vernacular" as a linguistic metaphor that presumes localisation precipitating out of "high" language use. "Demotic" points to a subaltern commonality that I think connects many global "popular" photographic practices.

It points to a horizontal, rather than the vertical space of the "vernacular".

I like to make my mark on texts (always in pencil and always in my own copies). I find these venatic marks and squiggles invaluable if subsequently I have the need to retrace my steps. Now that my home and office have both reached "peak book", I especially value small publications. I find myself resenting needlessly large volumes. Related to this I have long advocated that all publications should have a carbon footprint grading (indicating the ratio of valuable thinking contained relative to real world harm).

How significant are theories and histories of photography now that curation is so prominent?

More so than ever, especially since photography theory got interesting again (largely because of the provocations of Friedrich Kittler and Ariella Aïcha Azoulay, and the writing of Georges Didi-Huberman). Kittler's 'technomaterial' questions are bracing for anthropologists: he's both hilarious and scary. He pushes Roland Barthes' 'ontological desire' to destruction. I love his observation that 'doing media history is like learning higher mathematics by hearsay', although I obviously don't agree with it. I find the power of Didi-Huberman's writing in *Images in Spite of All* (2007) astonishing. His account of those four images from Auschwitz is an unforgettable affirmation of Barthes' point about the power of authentication exceeding the power of representation. Azoulay I admire for her political courage and for (at least in her early work) blowing open the Foucauldian/Taggian consensus. She has made it possible to think again about the ways in which power fears photography, and photography's unruliness and subversion.

What qualities do you admire in other writers?

There is a contradiction: I aspire to definite hypotheses that are "falsifiable" in a Popperian sense. But the writers I learn most from have imaginative strengths that are hardly "testable". I've always loved Benjamin's advice about looking not at what the neon sign says but at

     Christopher Pinney

'the fiery pool reflecting it in the asphalt': I want to gaze into the fiery pool and I think that's enabled by subtlety and ambivalence. Homi K. Bhabha is a writer I greatly admire, though I've come to view his work more and more as the specific application of general insights from Jacques Derrida. But alongside the ambivalence I really value empiricism and the discovery of things not previously known. As an anthropologist that means fieldwork, i.e. 24 hours immersion. The Chicago historian/anthropologist of India Bernard Cohn used to quote (R. H. Tawney, I think) to the effect that 'historians need stouter boots': I think photographic writers need them too. The Photodemos collective project *Citizens of Photography* is perhaps an example of this: it repositions Azoulay's argument about the political potential of photojournalism onto "demotic" practices and then aims to "test" them through ethnographic research (the collective consists of six of us working in Bangladesh, Cambodia, Greece, India, Nepal, Nicaragua, Nigeria and Sri Lanka). Thinking with Azoulay allowed us, among other things, to grasp how deeply photography engages subjunctive and proleptic futures rather than pasts.

Well Benjamin and Siegfried Kracauer remain enduring sources of insight: I find them completely inexhaustible. I recently started to read Ernst Bloch on 'colportage' and the 'un-contemporaneous'. But also Bhabha (for ambivalence and iteration), Friedrich Kittler (for Teutonic inflexibility), Carlo Ginzburg (for venatic and conjectural brilliance), J. M. Coetzee (for understanding mimesis as infection), Geeta Kapur (for her grip on the politics of surfaces), Karen Strassler (for beautiful ethnography), Georges Didi-Huberman (for the viscerality of the event) and Elizabeth Edwards (for insights into performance in the Torres Strait). Azoulay's work, especially *The Civil Contract of Photography* (2008) is of major importance. Among recent publications I admire are Miyarrka Media Collective's amazing *Phone and Spear* (2019), Sean Foley and Lukas Birk's *Indian Minute Camera Photographers* (2021) and Diwas Raja KC and Nepal Picture Library's *Dalit: A Quest for Dignity* (2018). Ashish Rajadhyaksha wrote an amazing article in 1987 that I still feel my work is in continuing conversation with. Maybe, above all, Barthes because I feel I've rediscovered him after dismissing him in line with the Taggian episteme. For every ludicrous observation in *Camera Lucida* (1980), there is a profound one.

Never really sure what "criticality" is unless it's the stuff that galleries pay for when you get commissioned to write a catalogue essay. I feel pretty alienated from that form of gravitas-jargonistic-puffery. I'm very keen on thinking, but that's something very different. I think every photography writer should be supplied with a basic emergency kit (Benjamin, a little bit of Kracauer and maybe some chocolate biscuits) and then ordered out into the world. Photography theory has paid too much attention to discourse and too little to practice. I suppose the desire for real-world engagement reflects my own 'ontological desire', to recall Barthes. We've had enough of – Barthes again – subjecting images to the 'civilised code of perfect illusions': photography's 'intractable reality' needs to be collided with the intractability of global practices and imaginaries.

Deborah Willis

Deborah Willis, PhD, is University Professor and Chair of the Department of Photography & Imaging at the Tisch School of the Arts at New York University, US. She is the recipient of the MacArthur Fellowship, a Guggenheim Fellowship and a member of the American Academy of Arts & Sciences. She is the author of The Black Civil War Soldier: A Visual History of Conflict and Citizenship *(NYU Press, 2021) and* Posing Beauty: African American Images from the 1890s to the Present *(W.W. Norton, 2009), amongst others.*

Professor Willis' curated exhibitions include Framing Moments: Photography from the Kalamazoo Institute of Arts *(Michigan, US, 2021);* Migrations and Meaning(s) in Art *(Maryland Institute College of Art, Baltimore, Maryland, US, 2020);* Reframing Beauty: Intimate Moments *(Indiana University, Bloomington, US, 2016);* Out [o] Fashion Photography: Framing Beauty *(Henry Art Gallery, Seattle, Washington, US, 2013) and* Let Your Motto Be Resistance: African American Portraits *(International Center of Photography, New York, 2007).*

I was introduced to photography at an early age because my dad was obsessed with his Rolleiflex camera and photographed the family often. My mother also had a beauty shop in our house. We had several picture magazines such as *Ebony*, *LOOK*, *LIFE* and *JET*. I think the epiphany was the culmination of all – family photographs, magazine images and discovery storytelling through photographs and I started writing as an undergraduate student at the Philadelphia College of the Arts in the mid-1970s.

What is your writing process?

No formal process that I see easy to reflect on, but I write in the mornings at daylight and through the afternoon. If I am writing about an artist or photographer, I research online and often connect through interviewing on the telephone. I read reference books that relate to the photographer's work and, if I am writing about my own work or an archive, I look closely at the works and reflect from memory or an event.

What are the questions or problems that motivate your writing?

I love aspects of storytelling that are personal that respond to joy. As a student, I missed stories that depicted the beauty of black culture and diverse stories of women and work. Ever the student of photography, I continued to notice gaps in relationship to women and their interests in the practice of photography and began asking questions about the multiple identities women and girls perform as they play and work. These are the experiences that motivate me to look at a photograph and begin to read the image from the subject in the foreground to the background… If it is a street scene or images on a wall, I am curious who 'curated' the home to allow it to appear safe or welcoming.

Can you say something about your use of different modes of writing and what they have been able to activate within the field, from academic art history to the first-person narratives of Picturing Us *(1994)?*

Memoir, fiction, historical fiction and free-flow narrative writing are all inspiring to me. What I enjoyed about contacting the diverse group of writers for *Picturing Us* was the ability to write a cohesive story that reimagined an image on page. It was magical to edit the works and feel the enthusiasm of each contributor as they reconsidered the importance of the visual experiences.

What kind of reader are you?

I am open to all – biographies and mysteries are foremost. I love reading Langston Hughes, Zora Neale Hurston, James Baldwin, Toni Morrison, Amy Tan, Danielle Steele and Agatha Christie all use historical narratives to tell their versions of fictions and aspects of truths.

How significant are theories and histories of photography now that curation is so prominent?

I continue to be inspired by the writings of Stuart Hall and his theories on visual culture. Liz Wells is central to my teaching and remains a go-to source for me as well as art historian Kellie Jones. I am inspired by the way Tina Campt has introduced a theory on 'listening' to images and Mark Sealy's 'decolonising' images. These experiences open up a plethora of ways in which one can bear witness to an image or experience. Photography has had a major impact on exposing the racially motivated murders in the 19th to the 21st centuries, the pandemic caused deaths and illnesses and activists striving for change here in the US and globally. Witnessing world events has become a process of self-reflection for me and having the opportunity to consider new photographic narratives about fashion, desire and loss in art journals and international magazines has been the most rewarding experience during the last 18 months.

What qualities do you admire in other writers?

Visualising a moment and translating the experience cogently onto the page. That excites me because it allows me to feel the magic of writing inspired by the imagination.

Toni Morrison wrote: 'I am a storyteller and therefore an optimist, a firm believer in the ethical bend of the human heart… from my point of view, your life is already artful – waiting, just waiting, for you to make it art.' I connected to this phrase when I read Morrison and Baldwin. Works by Maaza Mengiste, Robin Kelley, Edwidge Danticat, Okwui Enwezor, Carrie Mae Weems and Gordon Parks continue to influence me.

What is the place of criticality in photography writing now?

The impact of criticality is central to writing on photography at a time when migration, border crossings, memory and identities are being challenged and photographers are processing all these moments and writers are asking questions about notions of home and the significant ways black visual narratives respond to culture, politics and intimacy. The framework of criticality enables us to both reflect and imagine.

Max Houghton

Max Houghton is a writer, curator and editor working with the photographic image as it intersects with politics, law and human rights. She runs the MA in Photojournalism and Documentary Photography at London College of Communication, University of the Arts London, where she organises regular public talks, symposia and exhibitions. Her writing has appeared in publications by The Photographers' Gallery, London and the Barbican, London, as well as in the international arts press, including Foam, 1000 Words, Photoworks *and* Granta.
With Fiona Rogers, she is co-author of Firecrackers: Female Photographers Now *(Thames & Hudson, 2017).*
She is a Laws faculty scholarship doctoral candidate at University College London. With David Birkin, she is co-founder of research hub Visible Justice.

I had just finished the NCTJ (National Council for the Training of Journalists) course in 2001, and was researching (more than writing) for a *Guardian* journalist, Nick Davies, when Jon Levy, who'd I'd met through a mutual friend, asked if I'd write for his new website for photojournalists, *Foto8*. He sent me a set of photographs taken in Vietnam by an American photographer called Les Stone, which documented the ongoing transgenerational effects of Agent Orange. It was a fascinating exercise, because immediately I felt a responsibility to the overall subject matter of the Vietnam War, to the photographer and to the people in the pictures who I would never meet. Also, my question was: am I writing about the images or about the subject matter? These concerns endure. Six years later, I began an MA in critical theory (I didn't have a first degree) to help me think them through. *Foto8* grew from being a kind of dotcom start up to a published magazine, which eventually, along with Lauren Heinz, I edited. My bottom-line excitement, in staying with photographs for so long, is the idea that what we see never resides in what we say… It is an infinite relation, as Michel Foucault wrote. I'm always skipping from one register to the other, and back again.

What is your writing process?

My writing process is essentially reading, listening, editing, running and sleeping. I think that if we let it, our 'back brain' (please don't ask me for the science!) works it all out while we're doing other things. I can only understand something if I've written about it, or if I've been lucky enough to have a proper dialogic conversation on the subject. I'm not a hugely opinionated person, so it's important to afford very close attention to the work, and indeed to spend time with it, in order to find out what it might be that I think, or that the work emits.

What are the questions or problems that motivate your writing?

I'm interested in the idea of being able to write *with* photographs, which I hope might be a practice underpinned by an ethics of care. I think this is an originally feminist term, which resists patriarchal injustices… And while, of course, that is part of my intention, I also mean to use the term in relation to the root of the word 'curate' – *cura* – which is a specific way of paying attention. If I am asked to write with an artist's images, it is important to me to impart the same kind of care in my writing as the photographer did in the original images. I don't tend to write about work that doesn't move me; in that sense I'm not a critic at all, though I know there is useful place for such writing. I'm also motivated by what (photographic) images might do in the world, and in how, as technical images (as Vilém Flusser described them), they combine with other images in the world to stimulate thought processes. The image brings a different form of knowledge, which is different again when combined with text. It's fair to say the image-text is the underlying question that motivates my writing. As well as this, I'm always interested in what moves me; what connects me to actual feeling, and, as a logical extension of that, what might move others. At best, I hope my words might sometimes connect people to emotion. I think we can all exist very superficially. If we take time to notice how we feel, and when we feel, and manage not judge those feelings as 'good' or 'bad', we may be able to spend a little longer thinking about what matters. Finally, I continue to seek an inclusive practice, and my desire to challenge and refuse brutal, dangerous and often dominant power structures that shape our world remains potent.

What kind of reader are you?

Oh, reading. I don't know who or what or how I'd be without it. I wish I could read everything I want to read, but then I wouldn't live. It's simply how I understand the world; it's been my way of being in it all my life. I guess I'm *that* kind of reader!

How significant are theories and histories of photography now that curation is so prominent?

I'm not sure one precludes the other? I'm very glad to see how curatorial practice is expanding to unpick those questions that theories or histories might more traditionally cover, but surely they are all interwoven as discourses? Okwui Enwezor's 2002 documenta would offer a very significant example of such weaving for me, for example. I wonder if I fully understand the question? I certainly see how curation is influencing future theories and histories, even in terms of whose histories are being made visible. It's also an aspect of my way of being with photographs that recently I've been able to pursue, but this is not an isolated or removed practice… On the contrary…

Fiona's wonderful *Firecracker* platform rightly foregrounds the individual work of the artists, and I guess we were not seeking to make such a statement. I'm grateful for your phrasing; it's absolutely documentary that grounds me, but not in any kind of limited way. I see documentary as a desire to gain evidence of something vital, something that needs to be seen, shared and understood; afforded attention. Its methods can and indeed must be as expansive as possible. The kind of work that understands how documentary images have been used to categorise and control; the kind of work that has ingested some of the world's trillions of other images; the kind of work that seeks; the kind of work that may never even be finished… This is what interests me.

Clarity, (emotional) honesty, generosity, nuance, wit, precision, creating images through words, humility, mystery, playfulness (not necessarily all at once)… The same qualities I admire in other humans(!).

All works by W. G. Sebald, without question (though of course there ought always to be questions). T. S. Eliot's *Four Quartets* (1941). Foucault's *The Order of Things* (1966), Philippe Sands' *East West Street* (2016), Patricia J. Williams' *The Alchemy of Race and Rights* (1991). Emily Brontë's *Wuthering Heights* (1847), Roy de Carava and Langston Hughes' *The Sweet Flypaper of Life* (1955), James Agee and Walker Evans' *Let Us Now Praise Famous Men* (1941), bell hooks' *Teaching to transgress* (1994), Maurice Blanchot's *The Writing of the Disaster* (1980), "To See and Not See" (1993) by Oliver Sacks, "You're" (1960) by Sylvia Plath… I could go on…

Taco Hidde Bakker

Taco Hidde Bakker works as a writer, translator, teacher and curator in the field of the arts, specialising in photography. He studied painting at two art schools and obtained an MA in Photographic Studies at Leiden University, the Netherlands. He has contributed writing to numerous artist books, catalogues and magazines, amongst them Camera Austria International, Foam, The PhotoBook Review, British Journal of Photography *and* TRIGGER. *Bakker is the author of* The Photograph That Took the Place of a Mountain *(Fw:Books, 2018), a collection of essays and other writings on photographers and artists. He teaches Theory at the Utrecht University of the Arts, the Netherlands, and is a member of the research and curatorial collective Radical Reversibility.*

Not long before I started the MA Photographic Studies at Leiden University in 2005. About five years earlier, I had graduated from art school and had since worked as a painter, draughtsman and photographer (besides the occasional side-job). In art school, I did a basic course in photography (operating the analogue camera, developing film and printing in the darkroom). Although I'd been taking photographs since I was 16 or 17, I considered them as mere sketches or study material in the service of drawing and painting. However, only during the years of my own professional and artistic practice in photography did I begin to take the medium more seriously. It was then that I began to read and study several histories and theories of photography, probably from a wish to better understand the popularity of the medium and its many applications, also outside the arts. I desired to learn more about the medium in an organised way and was happy that I was accepted in this new programme at Leiden University, in the year that Susan Meiselas started guest teaching there as well. I connected well with Meiselas because of my internship at the arctic media collections at the National Museum of Ethnology in Leiden and my yearning to learn more about photography through anthropological perspectives. Other teachers responded well to my writing, which stimulated me to continue to relate to photographs (in their material manifestations) and photography (in its abstracted, theoretical dimensions) through the medium of writing.

I almost always feel in limbo about my "job description". In recent years, the emphasis has shifted towards teaching and curation, so I've added even more to the list. During the transitional phase from image-maker (visual artist and photographer) to someone circling around image projects in different guises, but rarely anymore as image producer, I was never sure of my exact role. Several roles would also sometimes overlap so that I just list multiple activities rather than trying to condense them into one epithet.

I've grown a bit hesitant to keep using this title explicitly. It somehow flows naturally from other activities, and builds upon knowledge and experience. I feel most confident as "sparring partner" when it happens in passing, when there's no immediate pressure to arrive at tangible results. In the absence of such pressure, I feel that I can honestly have a substantial conversation with a photographer or artist about their plans or work in progress and get a sense of what kind of materialisation and presentation the work asks for, so to say. There's not that much I can do after that besides sometimes, and preferably in passing too, connecting the artist to other people who could be of help in bringing the body of work (or project) further, such as image editors, writers, graphic designers, curators, publishers… In some cases, I remain connected as a sounding board and/or writer. To be able to follow developments from early stages onward is like being a "participant observer", being engaged yet remaining at a sufficient critical distance in order to be able to write freely.

It all depends on the purpose of the writing. I don't have any thought-out writing strategies. Almost every piece of my published writing comes from assignments, whether self-initiated or by invitation. It's paradoxical that the more I've been writing and publishing the harder it seems for me to write. In the beginning, I could be propelled by some kind of naïve energy and have pieces published without much editorial consideration. Today, I'm mostly interested in finding a mode of writing and a form for the text that I feel is appropriate to the artist or photographer's work. In that sense, I'm writing not so much *about* as *in conversation with…*
    In terms of process, I can discern a few common themes: if the artist is alive I wish to have a conversation, whether in person, on the phone, over Zoom or otherwise. During or shortly after that conversation, I take notes, mostly in shorthand. Then, I'm trying to

gauge my response, to the person and the work. I'd also like to know a few things about someone's background and interests, to what extent and how that influences a life, a worldview, and the visual work of course. If time allows, I like to study some materials (books, films, lectures and so on) pertaining to their work, especially so if I don't know much about the theme(s) at hand. The next step is to become aware of the type of publication and its intended audience, as this shapes the genre, the style and tone of voice of the writing. Within certain parameters I try to find or negotiate as much room to experiment as possible.

What are the questions or problems that motivate your writing?

Usually, the writing process itself functions as the catalyst that brings up certain questions and problems or shapes them into sharper relief. I'm mostly guided by an inquisitive and open attitude, and like to have images and projects guide me into unknown, or half-known, territory. There's always the image-word issue, as probably every writer on imagery recognises and with which some photographers and artists feel uncomfortable. What kind of writing does justice to the work in question? Which words are appropriate? The writing literally provides con*text*, frames the imagery linguistically and conceptually. The question of *how* to respond to work permeates each and every piece of my writing. In recent years, there's basically one problem that haunts me, and that I've difficulties with in expressing: namely the all-pervasive question of how the warming climate changes everything, including the way images and the imagination are implicated in this 'policy problem from hell', as Anthony Leiserowitz from the Yale Program on Climate Change Communication succinctly called it.

The transformations in our climate seem to hold some particular problems for our image world, concerned as it is with quickness and spectacle. How does photography and writing begin to adequately address this?

What if photography and writing are part of the problem? I'm afraid there's plenty of photography and writing that's complicit, and if not explicitly so, then subconsciously triggering the mimetic machine that drives copycat behaviour. I would need to write (or curate) a book to analyse such questions, but the current predicament invites me to first question the fundamental formats of "normal" production and distribution. Is writing or photography even necessary? And why then a book? As habitual, path-dependent animals, often choosing the easy way (cheap comfort that in the longer run proves disruptive and destructive) and instant gratification over ecological sound ideals, we get stuck in the grooves playing the same old tunes over and over again. But since the warming climate is on course to changing everything resulting in many unforeseen and incalculable consequences – and since the Earth's biosphere is a rather complex whole – we better allow ourselves to fundamentally revise what we've come to take for granted. For that, we need courageous and imaginative thinking and acting, that in part can be inspired by writing and photography, but likely not in shapes and structures that fit into received ideas about what good writing and photography entails.

Perhaps we need less photography and less writing and cultivate what psychologist J.J. Gibson names 'ecological perception' – a subtle mode of sensory perception that's guided by an organism's immersion and movements within an environment. Walter Benjamin already noted in the 1920s that the speed of industrial technologies and modern media puts enormous pressure on experience. Without experience, there can be no true storytelling, only disembodied entertainment. One common deficient of photography and writing might be that they both overstimulate our visual faculty, to the detriment of the other senses. With our research and curatorial collective Radical Reversibility, we tried to address these issues in a group show called *From Seeing to Acting* (held at Looiersgracht 60 in Amsterdam in 2021), where we showed experimental photo and video works alongside sculpture, installation, drawings (including a drawing being made blindfolded during the show in dialogue with visitors), sound and scent. Our written exhibition concept was somewhat poetic and cryptic, but one curator and writer who'd experienced the show at least twice told us that "one could feel the concept", which we took as a compliment.

In short, coming back to your question, to adequately begin to address the climate crisis I think means we better start fundamentally scrutinising the roles of the very forms and formats we use to address this crisis, as well as question our ridiculously high collective image output. The way forward into nature may mean both reviving ancient forms (like oral storytelling, poetry, singing, weaving, ritual performances and so on), yet grafting them onto – and mixing them with – advanced technologies. Nevertheless, slowing down and producing and consuming less is never a bad thing.

What kind of reader are you?

A promiscuous reader! I always carry a hodgepodge of books, magazines and papers around or with me (in Dutch, English and German). There's rarely ever a dull moment in my reading life. Often, I'm reading multiple books simultaneously, from non-fiction (popular science, philosophy, (art) history, politics, memoir, essay) to poetry and fiction, recently also including science fiction. I cannot read too much fiction at the same time, as I find it quite demanding to surrender myself to fictional characters and settings, but I can read non-fiction (a misnomer) like we switched from one domain to the next every class hour in high school. I'm taking notes on little scraps of paper, in notebooks or in my writing application, Scrivener, which I mostly use as an advanced note-taking and note-organising tool. Just the act of taking notes helps to remind the most important lessons I got from the reading experience. It's hard for me to also keep up with all the writing in the realm of photography and other visual cultures. I'm rather selective there, to a large extent guided by happenstance, or by my quest to find relevant, topical writing for my students.

How significant are theories and histories of photography now that curation is so prominent?

Histories and theories of photography are forms of curation, too. They are about selecting, arranging, annotating and caring for what the "curator" finds worth passing on. The formats have changed and diversified, with, for example, multimedia exhibitions and online presentations, and I consider those to be shaping histories and theories as much as older forms such as essays and monographs, the latter of course relying more heavily on (written) discourse.

In your book The Photograph That Took The Place of A Mountain *(2018), you begin the collection of essays by focusing on three writers: Vilém Flusser, Peter Geimer and Ariella Aïcha Azoulay. Can you say something about this triad of thinkers? It seems like you are setting*

Yes, I wanted to open my curated volume – collecting 20 pieces of
writing from about a decade of writing around photography or photo-
related visual art – with three book reviews I had published earlier
of contemporary thinkers on photography. Reading their work had
at least co-shaped (or reshaped) my thinking about the medium.
By no means was I planning to replace the classic triad of writers
(Benjamin, Barthes, Sontag) with a new one. I think what Flusser,
Geimer and Azoulay had to offer were questions that I found more
urgent than the thematic angles of earlier generations of writers on
the medium. Azoulay and Geimer seem complementary, now that I
come to think of it, in their emphasis on the radical instability of the
medium (counterintuitive to the popular notion of photography as
'fixing' an image); Azoulay from the standpoint of meaning and context
(analysing and speculating on the revolutionary democratic and human
rights potential of photography) and Geimer from the standpoint of the
essentially unstable materiality of images.

Flusser's thinking on photography, on the other hand, is much
more abstract and speculative, but since his thinking developed
on par with developments in computer and information technology,
his writings are interesting to read in the light of current questions
surrounding 'machine vision' and 'automated seeing'. The German
film essayist Harun Farocki, who happened to have filmed an interview
with Flusser, is also an early pioneer in reflecting on developments
in automated image recognition. In my view, his pertinent *Images
of the World and the Inscription of War* (1988) is a must-see for any
photography and visual studies student.

With students, I prefer to read writers who are also practicing
artists, for example Hito Steyerl and Trevor Paglen, or theorists like
Nicholas Mirzoeff, whose *How to See the World* (2015) is an accessible
analysis of, and introduction to, visual culture today, which nicely
maps current topics onto earlier issues and images.

Playfulness, curiosity, adventure and a light touch of madness.
Qualities I admire which I do not believe myself to possess are

rigorous and extensive research and the ability to write about complex issues in fluent, accessible prose.

I find influences hard to trace. Perhaps it's easiest to mention a few writers that I've read early (during the times of my studies) and that I feel partly stimulated my own writing, even though I don't aspire to match them, such as the French experimental novelist Georges Perec, the Soviet-Russian novelist Andrey Platonov (his fantastic *Chevengur* from 1928 must be one of the best novels I have ever read), and the Jewish Brazilian writer Clarice Lispector. Within my own domain, I admire the daring explorations of Flusser and the probing studies of Georges Didi-Huberman. They've both influenced me in different ways, although I cannot say that they've influenced my writing style. I've also learned a thing or two about seeing from poets, of whom I admire Wallace Stevens, Paul Celan and Francis Ponge amongst others.

I prefer to conceive of 'criticality' not as nominalisation but as attitude and action, so I prefer to think of "it" as a verb. What does it mean *to criticise* and if we decide that it's important indeed, how should we go about it? For one thing, any writing that is not meant to sell things displays critical thinking in the sense of making distinctions and pointing the reader to aspects and contexts the writer deems important (whether the writer is conscious of it or not).

The tasks facing us now and in the generations to come are enormous. Currently, I'm of the opinion that any critical writing (on photography or otherwise) that does not in one way or another contribute to (or call for) restoring and healing the rather lopsided (and *critically* dangerous) relationship between humans and the biosphere, is mere idleness. I'm also still publishing writings (usually on assignment, so they pay the bills) that don't yet quite live up to this demanding ideal, so I've got work to do on restoring the balance.

Wu Hung

Wu Hung holds the Harrie A. Vanderstappen Distinguished Service Professorship at the Department of Art History and the Department of East Asian Languages and Civilisations at the University of Chicago, US, where he is also the director of the Center for the Art of East Asia and the Adjunct Curator at the Smart Museum. An elected member of the American Academy of Art and Science and awarded with an Honorary Degree from Harvard University, he sits on many international committees including Guggenheim Museum's Asian Art Council, and chairs the Academic Committee of the OCAT Museum Group. Wu Hung has received many awards for his publications and academic services, including the 2018 Distinguished Scholar Award and the 2022 Distinguished Lifetime Achievement Award for Writing on Art, both from the College Art Association of America (CAA).

Wu Hung's research interests include both traditional and contemporary art, and he has published many books and curated many exhibitions in these two fields. His interdisciplinary interests have led him to experiment with different ways to tell stories about Chinese art, as exemplified by Monumentality in Early Chinese Art and Architecture *(Stanford University Press, 1995);* The Double Screen: Medium and Representation of Chinese Pictorial Art *(University of Chicago Press, 1996);* Remaking Beijing: Tiananmen Square: the Creation of a Political Space *(University of Chicago Press, 2005);* A Story of Ruins: Presence and Absence in Chinese Art and Visual Culture *(Princeton University Press, 2012) and* Zooming In: Histories of Photography in China *(University of Chicago Press, 2016).*

I started writing about photographs quite late in my career, in the late 1990s after I had received tenure. I was trained as an historian of Chinese art. The books I published before 1996 all dealt with pre-modern art – ritual vessels, monuments and pictorial medium and representation. Photography attracted me via two paths. First, when I started curating exhibitions of contemporary Chinese art and writing about this art in the late 90s, I discovered that photography was one of the most dynamic branches in this art and deeply enmeshed with painting, performance art, Body Art, Conceptual Art, and so on. Secondly, when I began working on a book about "ruins" in Chinese art and visual culture, I realised that the introduction of photography in the 19th century radically changed how Chinese people and artists perceived and represented the world. At that point, I also began to develop other research projects on historical photographs along two intertwining lines, which I call "Chinese photography" and "photography in China". The former is an integral component of modern Chinese visual culture, while the latter, though produced in China and featuring Chinese subjects, served external agendas.

What is your writing process?

With contemporary photography, most of the time I'm first captured by particular images in exhibitions and publications, which lead me to their creators. I interview them, befriend them and conduct research on their entire corpus of works, before I sit down to write about them.

With historical photography, my interests are typically aroused by archival materials that pose unanswered questions. One example is my study of Milton Miller's Chinese portraits which he made in Hong Kong around 1860. I was intrigued by these photos when I studied them in the Getty Research Institute because they confronted me with many questions which I couldn't answer: Who are the anonymous sitters in the pictures? Are these images really "portraits" in a conventional sense? Why did Miller make these photos in the first place? I spent several years to find the answers to these questions.

In your writing on Miller and on early photography, you advocate for a form of intense looking and reading.

Although looking at old photographs and writing about them are not the same thing, they are certainly related to each other. For one thing, both unfold in time. Intense looking is a temporal process through which the researcher "enters" into the picture and tries to see it from within – to discover *significant details* from a historical point of view. Writing translates this visual undertaking – if it is successful – into a written form. But the sense of discovery can still help animate the written words and bring readers on an exploratory visual journey.

What are the questions or problems that motivate your writing?

One set of problems is concerned with the history, status, motivation and function of contemporary Chinese "experimental" photography, which developed into a strong trend in China from the 1980s onward. Instead of perceiving and interpreting this trend as an anonymous movement, I'm more interested in discovering the experiences and experiments of individual photographic artists. To me, the differences between these artists, rather than their commonalities, should remain at the centre of investigation and presentation.

Another set of questions is related to the historical relationship between photography and Chinese art and visual culture. In particular, how did this modern technology change people's perception of the world and of themselves, as revealed by the emergence of new kinds of images in the second half of the 19th century and later. For example, images of architectural ruins emerged for the first time in Chinese art; new types of portraiture and self-portraiture also appeared (such as inscribed photos I have termed "I-Portraits"). These new images often coincided with seminal historical events.

A third set of problems is even broader and focuses on the general relationship between photography, painting and objects. This is the central thread of my forthcoming book *The Full-length Mirror: A Global Visual History* (the 2021 Chinese version is titled *Object · Painting · Photography: A Global History of the Full-length Mirror*). A photograph is both an image and a material construct, and it represents objects in specific ways. While photography and painting are similar in this respect, they also differ in ontology and in the correlation between image and material.

Moreover, a more complex story about the relationship of photography, painting and objects begins to emerge when we observe this relationship in a global context.

I read mainly around specific research/writing projects. Since I usually conduct two, three or even four projects simultaneously, more often than not I read books and articles on unrelated subjects at the same time. This also means that I read more for work than for pleasure. I don't consider this an enviable habit.

I am, by training, an historian of images, and my writing and curatorial projects usually have strong historical frameworks. Even for those on contemporary art, including photography, I feel that I need to understand and present historical contexts, which can be artistic, intellectual, cultural and political, and to have a firm grasp of how a photographer's artistic development is interwoven with their life experiences. In a broad sense all of these can be called "historical".

In terms of theory, I prefer not to rely on preconceived theories, understood as self-sustaining discourses with their own intellectual context, in developing curatorial and writing projects. To me, "concepts" are more productive because these projects always need certain conceptual frameworks. Four years ago, my colleagues and I at Beijing's OCAT Institute started an annual competition called "Research-Oriented Curatorial Projects", encouraging young curators to organise exhibitions that combine serious research and theoretical thinking. There have been a good number of successful examples. But many submissions fall back on well-known (Western) theories as preexisting parameters, either applying them to interpreting artworks or illustrating them with selected examples. The "Research-Oriented Curatorial Projects" programme tries to counter this tendency which has become widespread in the field.

Yes, a historical photograph is never transparent and displays its "meaning" on the surface because of its inevitable dehistoricisation: it has lost its original associations with its time, place and people. In other words, it has "survived" history to become something else. Verbal description of the image alone can tell us little about its historical meaning. But sensitive observations are crucial for a researcher to discover *problems*, which then stimulate further investigations. I consider this process of finding, observing, describing and investigating a combined creative exercise, regardless whether it can produce a definite conclusion. My writing and curatorial projects more or less follow this logic, but curatorial projects naturally also demand taking into consideration the logic and functionality of the exhibition space.

What qualities do you admire in other writers?

Real understanding of the subject. Clarity. Being engaging. Passion. An interest in new ways of telling a story.

Do writings from beyond photography also influence how you think about the photographic image? Approaching photography from an oblique angle can also be a revealing strategy.

In thinking about photography? It should be *Camera Lucida* (1980), like with many of us. I also want to mention Walter Benjamin's "The Little History of Photography" (1931), which says that a photograph has something in it which 'goes beyond testimony to the photographer's art.' In saying this, Benjamin means those things which a photograph doesn't display on the surface but which are nevertheless there, arousing curiosity or even fantasy. I feel that this is especially true for historical photographs, which always go "beyond" the images themselves, compelling historians to pursue the missing information.

I take "criticality" as reflections – through either words or images – on photography itself. As such, criticality is always important to photography writing, although it doesn't have to be externalised as the sole or main purpose. In my mind, the best photography writing – or writing on any type of image – should simultaneously expose hidden meanings of images and articulate new ways of arriving at such meanings. *Camera Lucida* again provides a supreme example.

Tanvi Mishra

Tanvi Mishra is based in New Delhi, India, and works with images as a photo editor, curator and writer. Amongst her interests are South Asian visual histories, representation within image-making as well as the notion of fiction in photography, particularly in the current political landscape.

Until recently, she was the Creative Director of The Caravan, *a journal of politics and culture published out of Delhi. She is part of the photo-editorial team of* PIX *and works as an independent curator forming part of the curatorial teams of Photo Kathmandu, Nepal, Delhi Photo Festival and BredaPhoto Biennial, the Netherlands (2022). She has served on multiple juries, including World Press Photo, Chennai Photo Biennale Photo Awards and the Catchlight Global Fellowship. She has also been a mentor for the* Women Photograph *programme and is part of the first international advisory committee of World Press Photo. Mishra is also serving as the curator of the Louis Roederer Discovery Award at Les Rencontres d'Arles 2023, France.*

Some of her recent writing includes "Viral Images: The role of photography in documenting India's COVID-19 disaster" (The Caravan, 2021); "Photography in Crisis: Repurposing the Medium for Solidarity and Action" (Foam, 2020); "The New Era of South Asian Photography Festivals" (Aperture, 2021); "Archive as Companion: text accompanying Priya Kambli's work 'Buttons for Eyes'" (PIX Vol. 18 Passages, 2022); "The Great Upheaval: Can the digital revolution potentially shift the power dynamic in photography?" (Viewbook Transformations, 2017). She has also contributed to books including WHY EXHIBIT: Positions on exhibiting photographies *(FW: Books, 2018) and exhibition catalogues such as* Taxed to the Max *(Noordelicht International Photography Festival, 2020).*

A little more than a decade ago, I was invited to join the team of *PIX*, an editorial and curatorial practice aimed at building an archive of contemporary photography in South Asia. For the publication, *PIX* solicits lens-based works, and pairs them with writing that responds to the images. At this point, I was establishing my photographic practice, and negotiating my relationship with the medium. I thought of myself as solely a photographer, and believed that the core of the practice was animated by those who made images. My work at *PIX* signified my first professional interaction with the work of others, no longer as just a viewer, but as an interlocutor, an editor and a collaborator. The sustained engagement with other makers and their practices played a crucial role in the evolution of my own practice as well. Through this process I was introduced, or rather coerced, into writing.

I have always found it easier to speak with photographs. Through many years of crafting visual stories, initially as a photographer but largely as an editor, I have become, somewhat, attuned to the rhythms of weaving images into compelling narratives. The trajectory of arriving at this point of "ease" has been somewhat predictable, and regularly working the muscle has made the photo-editing process feel more natural. I approached writing with a greater reluctance – my relationship with it continues to be complicated, but it has helped me give shape and voice to the ideas marinating in my mind. In my earliest published piece, for instance, in 2012, in writing about the artists featured in a volume of *PIX*, I was forced to articulate my photo-editorial choices into words. This was the first time that I crystallised the process of editing images, inherently abstract and intuitive, into concrete sentences. Since then, this connection – between my practice of writing and editing of photographs – has been constantly reinforced, and one has continued to inform and enrich the other.

Over the years, my writing on the work of photographers has ranged from conversational essays to commentary and analytical pieces. As my practice developed, the work that I was commissioned for became more wide-ranging. I was invited to comment on larger questions looming over the visual medium, reflecting on its theoretical and conceptual framework, as well as examining the contours of the industry and the fault lines that continued to plague it. Since I work primarily as an editor of images, these "prompts" that came my way in the form of writing assignments shaped the trajectory of my writing practice.

During my years at *The Caravan*, a long-form journal of politics and culture, my writing was heavily influenced by the magazine and its editorial process. It is here that the prompts shifted – from premises assigned by others – to my own responses to themes we were engaging with in the newsroom. While my interests are medium-specific, I am drawn now to the intersection of the image with politics, culture and society. In how images circulate within larger publics, and how that affects our ways of being as citizens in this world.

My process is often marked by tedium – it can be terribly slow, frustrating and one that mandates constant revision.

I rarely ever write "for myself", though that is a direction I wish to desperately move towards. Most of my writing is done on a fairly urgent timeline – either in response to a commission or to an unfolding event. My experience in journalism instilled the belief that getting a piece published at the right moment is as crucial to its reception and circulation, as chiselling it to "perfection". Since writing is the part of my practice, I am least confident and most unsure about, if left to myself, I can continue to endlessly tweak and tighten, in an attempt to reach the best possible conclusion. Even though the lack of time can feel constraining at the time of shaping a piece, it is also an immensely powerful impetus in releasing my writing out into the world. I am learning to get comfortable with the idea that some of the most compelling writing does not necessarily present normative resolutions or answers, but it offers instead, a space to question, stir debate and generate ideas.

The physical act of writing feels burdened with procrastination. I inevitably delay the *start* till the last possible moment, perhaps because of the potent anxiety I continue to experience on encountering an empty page. However, the *process* of writing begins much earlier. In the days leading up to putting words to paper (or a Word document!), I make my way through the premise and arguments in response to the prompt. A lot of this thinking happens in the unlikeliest of places – on a walk, in the shower, while cooking – and rarely at my work desk. On the days when I am actually writing, I am fairly chaotic. I have many books and multiple tabs open, because I comb through references fairly extensively. Most of these are texts I have read before, and that have offered insights that resonate with the idea I am working through. Other sources of inspiration tend to be authors or thinkers whose words help me when I arrive at an impasse. I find myself to be both heavily distracted, fielding multiple influences at the same time and intensely concentrated, in that I cannot pursue any other intellectual task during those days.

My writing process is quite similar to my photo-editing practice: with a large set of images for instance, the beginning can often feel quite scattered, and the ideas and arguments fairly disconnected. It is somewhere at the half-way mark of the process that the links and connections begin to emerge in the loose structure, revealing a possible outcome where the whole is greater than the sum of its parts. Sometimes, the emergence of this clarity can hasten the process, and the remaining puzzle is solved at an accelerated pace. Just as with an edit on images, writing benefits with some resting time, allowing the words to sit next to each other, revealing meanings that were perhaps not as visible the first time around.

I wonder if you might expand on the "prompt" as you describe it: it seems to be a catalyst and a beginning, of course, but I wonder if in some ways, it is also for you a sign of writing's contingency, something which describes how, as a writer, you are always in dialogue from the very beginning. Does your attention to the "prompt" describe something of your writing practice and your attention to writings relationships?

I see the "prompt" as an impetus, one that pushes me to act. Those of us who choose to think of ourselves as political beings respond to change in our environment. Our craft is one way to channel this response.

The dialogue you speak of is ongoing, and inevitable. We use the tools we have at hand to articulate our concerns. For me, writing may fill in for the inadequacies, or limitations for response, within photography, or it may be used to activate different audiences.

I consider myself fortunate to be able to engage with the image in varied forms. This engagement is what I see as the dialogue – at times collaborating with image-makers, their work and archives and in other instances, using writing as a possible instrument of inquiry. I find this response to be contingent, and writing as one form of that contingency.

Most of what motivates my writing is what motivates my work with images. These concerns shift with time, in response to unfolding events and my evolving personal politics. I see writing as a way to distil the varied questions and ideas that emerge during my primary practice of working as a photo editor and curator.

Currently, one of the biggest questions I am wrestling with in photography is to do with the process by which images make their way into the world, and the manner in which their circulation shapes discourse – within the image economy, but particularly outside it, in society. I am interested in how the surplus of imagery affects our psychological being and how the consumption of these images moulds our reception to social, political or cultural realities.

Having worked in journalism, particularly on the photo and multimedia desks, I have witnessed the impacts of such circulation first hand. The choices we made had the potential to shape public opinion. This was both a potent instrument, as well as a heavy responsibility. While it may sound staid as a concept in the space of photo discourse, I am interested in the image as evidence in today's media landscape. Where does such evidence hold value, when courts themselves look away? How is media, and the narratives it is composed of, used as information warfare, both by those in power and those opposing it? How does the image need to be packaged to be consumed as truth or propaganda? How do we read political photographic fiction in today's image world? How do we decide to trust a certain image, or the sources it is disseminated through, and what governs this psychological response? When does image circulation, particularly on social media, trigger a near immediate reaction, whether by the general public or by organised troll armies? It is this response that I'm interested in examining: is it genuine or manufactured; how does it measure "truth"; how do these images change in their meaning as they further circulate in the digital realm?

Another concern that consumes much of my thinking is around the politics of representation – specifically, whether it is possible to ever circumvent the hierarchies and power dynamics embedded within photography. While, earlier, I was curious about how the "democratisation" of the medium impacted this balance, I am no longer as interested in the pervasiveness of and access to the medium, but more so in where this conversation around representation – "who gets to tell whose story" – leads us. The push towards local and "insider" narratives is one that is now, rightfully so, valued. This reorientation is the long-due reparation of the historically skewed representation of many communities and issues, which was a direct outcome of the privilege of either the coloniser's lens or the "outsider's" festishistic gaze.

However, I question the notion of this "insider" and how we arrive at its definition. Is there an ideal insider? Is she always best positioned to tell that story? Aren't we all insiders, truly, only to our own stories? And yet, autobiographical narratives are only a part of how we learn about the world, and how we choose to produce or consume media. Lived experience is a crucial component, in that it brings to the fore a gaze that is less essentialist than what has existed largely in narrative storytelling. We are, often, better placed to access communities or issues that we have engaged with otherwise, outside of the "professional" demand; those that we resonate or connect with as individuals or citizens, not necessarily only when tasked with representing them. Does this mean that there is a possibility for an honest engagement, that may well be "imperfect", with a narrative outside of the lived-experience paradigm? Is authentic storytelling a function of provenance? Is identity an absolute construct, or does it shift in response to the subject and landscape? I am interested in how the intersection of various markers like gender, caste, class, region, religion as well as traits such as lived experience and personal politics guide the making of this definition, complicate notions of identity and affect the proposition of narratives distinct from historically dominant perspectives. These intersections often guide the choices of artists I write about, and that writing is an important conduit that enables the development of my own understanding of the concerns regarding authorship and narrativising.

Recently, I have been interested in reflecting on the positionality of image-makers, and how their own identity impacts the work they put out into the world. The term "identity" here is not to be seen as synonymous with nationalistic definitions – defined by borders and passports – but more by their position as citizens in the world social order, and in relation to the narratives they construct. Whether it is even possible for works to reckon with aspects of the makers' identities and if so, whether photographic works are as much about the authors as they are about those who are photographed?

Within this realm lies one of my biggest concerns of late –
photography's inability, or limited ability, to shift the gaze towards the
perpetrator, the oppressor, the coloniser. These definitions are not in
relation to the conventional binaries of the West/East, urban/rural etc.,
but with reference to where the author of a work is placed when she
is representing someone other than herself. While contemporary
discourse has compelled narratives to shift, from unidimensional
perspectives of suffering and impact, to include a broader spectrum
of human emotion and experience, photography has been limited in
visualising those other than the victims or survivors. There has been an
inherent difficulty in exhibiting structures of supremacy, of complicity.

My own position as a dominant caste individual from India makes
this particularly pertinent for me. The need to pass the lens, and so the
power, into the hands of the oppressed and marginalised to build their
own narratives – of both joy and suffering – to self-represent their own
communities is urgent. But, alongside, authors, especially from
majoritarian or dominant identities, need to apply a more critical gaze
to their own communities – those, for instance, that have historically
oppressed others by way of privilege afforded by the caste system,
a discriminatory social order of hierarchy prevalent across the
subcontinent. The capacity of visual narratives to critique these
systems of power, and not merely display them as "documentation",
is rare in our image world. I am interested in these limitations and in
examining whether photography truly has the ability to upend
historical narratives, which have inevitably been authored by the very
dominant systems and lenses it has failed to effectively illustrate.

Apart from these conceptual interests, a lot of my writing is
motivated by visual works emanating from South Asia, particularly
when their vocabularies are distinct from mainstream photographic
canons. Since most references within photography are from Western
histories and contexts, I am drawn to artists and works that attempt to
break this trajectory in form and language. I usually engage with the
artists in an editorial or curatorial capacity, and the writing emerges
from these collaborations.

*Your description of the image as evidence feels
important, in that it gives an equal weight to how the
image is made and also put to use, how it acts and
impacts, alongside what it shows. Do you think this
process of exploring positionalities leads us in some*

ways towards images being understood as assemblages, and truth as something that cannot be reduced down to one essentialising characteristic?

The relationship between the photograph and "truth" has been a complicated one. Ambiguous by nature, the image has always been open to a subjective interpretation, even in its use as a document. As an editor, I particularly appreciate the transformation of an image and its meaning, when it interacts with another image, or with text; how it is re-casted depending on where it is placed, how it is disseminated and so on. The notion of "truth" has always been defined by multiple forces, at times by a collection of images, at times by other interactions and factors. What an assemblage may do, particularly in the case of evidentiary images, is to make a particular truth harder to deny. While an "iconic image", a term I find to be redundant now, may evince a particular truth about a situation by a singular author, the streams of images generated may help reiterate its evidentiary value.

However, as I write this, I find exceptions emerge to this proposition. Take the recent pull-out of the US from Afghanistan or the current war in Ukraine. What we see, despite the surfeit of images generated, is largely a singular perspective. A singular truth? The collections that emerge are predominantly authored by Western image-makers, or for Western publications. This repetition leads to a redundancy, with most photographers creating work that reaches the same conclusion. Rarely do we come across the deployment of the image in critiquing the systems that led to these conflicts, to look at the complicity of Western nations and modern-day cycles of imperialism.

In the case of positionalitics, I am not so concerned with this notion of "truth" but more with the aspect of authenticity, of honesty. Exploring an author's position in their work helps us parse through their motivations. Self-reflexivity can serve as an anchor, from which we construct our truths and reveal why we reach the conclusions we do.

What kind of reader are you?

Sporadic and unstructured. I now read mostly for work, which fortunately for me is around themes that genuinely interest me and enrich both my writing and image editing. Much of it is triggered through prompts – figuring my way through a writing invitation, working through an edit or deconstructing a premise someone may have posed. Often, reading offers me an articulation of a politics that I find difficult to put into words myself.

During my tenure at *The Caravan*, my role required extended reading from a wide spectrum of contributors spanning a range of topics. A lot of my writing education has been from observing their first drafts take shape into finessed final pieces. I was privy to the writer-editor dynamic and the tense tug of the relationship. I would pore over the comments from editors to the writers, and witness the evolution of these drafts, as they were refined over time, through intervention and exchange.

I always have a list of pending readings – which seems to grow at a much faster pace than the rate at which I consume them – and I'm constantly dreaming of a reading residency that may give me the time to catch up!

My engagement with the medium began as an image-maker. While my role may have changed significantly over the years, my understanding of photography is largely shaped through a practitioner's lens. I have never had any formal training in photographic education, and theory has never been a core component of my work with images.

That being said, I do consume some theoretical texts, particularly those that break away from being dense and opaque – the most common obstacle of this genre of writing. I do wrestle with the codification that theory brings with it, particularly for culture, and a medium as inherently ambiguous as photography. I have regard for theory and academia, for its rigour of thought and deep, sustained engagement. However, I am interested in working at the cusp of academia and practice. For this, theory needs to be activated into accessible forms and for academics to invest in dissemination across channels beyond their own structures. To quote from scholar Ruth Wilson Gilmore: 'to think theoretically, but speak practically.' I am drawn to artists/practitioners who comment on or respond to theory in their works, building additional channels of circulation and deconstruction.

As for histories of photography, I consume them to keep pace and build context to certain discussions or texts I come across. However, I approach these with some degree of caution, given that no history is definitive and mainstream versions have, largely, been authored by dominant perspectives. I am also constantly trying to strengthen these muscles of criticality, in order to allow an evolution of these definitions of who/what constitutes a dominant/mainstream or oppressed/fringe perspective, and that these can shift depending on relational dynamics. Largely, histories of photography – inevitably mimicking social histories – are rooted in Western canons and colonial perspectives. While they help build structures to understand *one* linear progression of the medium, they carry with them significant erasures, by missing out on or misrepresenting large populations and perspectives. I do advocate that some of them be read so as to have a framing, from which to subvert. Ariella Aïcha Azoulay's recent publication *Potential History: Unlearning Imperialism* (2019) is one such proposition for subversion, offering the possibility of an alternate reading of photography through historical time. Tina M. Campt's *Listening to Images* (2017) proposes using sound and haptics as a register to re-read images that have historically carried different meanings. I also consider micro-histories or personal histories as potent historical documents, if collated and contextualised within a historical timeline.

Then, it is predictable that my personal view of curation is not dependant on theories and histories of photography. I have always found them to be separate fields, that at some points may collide or intersect, and at others may run parallel or even be entirely removed from one another. I think the choice depends on the curator and/or the institution, depending on how they perceive a "valid" curatorial practice.

I consider curation to be as open-ended as an artist's practice – some may interpret it through a reliance on pedagogy, others may be influenced by theory without deploying it consciously in the building of work and even others may entirely reject it, dismissing it as didactic to build a curatorial premise on an entirely different tenor.

So, to answer the question, I don't find the link between theory, histories and curation to always be very direct or consistent to comment on how the supposed amplification of one impacts the other.

What qualities do you admire in other writers?

Accessibility, and the ability to weave complex ideas into simple sentences.

Brevity, precision, and narrative clarity.

An ability to be self-reflexive.

Personality, colour and texture in writing without deploying complicated language or purple prose.

I don't think I can name texts, because I associate more with authors and their trajectories of thought, than a particular iteration. It is simpler for me to list writers who have had some form of influence or provided inspiration, either to my politics or my practice. The connection is as intuitive as the one between multiple images during an editing exercise.

Listing them in no particular order: Tina M. Campt, Ariella Aïcha Azoulay, Mark Sealy, B. R. Ambedkar, Frantz Fanon, Kajri Jain, Maaza Mengiste, Teju Cole, Alana Hunt, David Campany, bell hooks, Amitava Kumar, Aveek Sen, Allan Sekula, Stuart Hall, Gayatri Gopinath, Audrey Lorde, Joan Didion, Joan Fontcuberta, Eyal Weizman.

Significant.

I do think that many texts in photography, are *about* images or descriptive writing. A lot of my own writing also falls within this definition, particularly when I am focusing on a specific artist's practice. While I am in favour of using writing to deconstruct image-making for a general public, and offer them a vocabulary with which to enter the work, I do not believe that a text must decode or lay bare the entire work to the audience. This would be an injustice to the image, to rob it of the ambiguity that makes it universal, in the way in which it connects to each individual.

Critical writing, however, allows an engagement that has the potential to "expand out of" the artists' practice, using it as a trigger to deconstruct an imposed premise or to weigh it against its own claims. It could also be used as a springboard to speak about larger themes – the image as a sociological study, or more formal, medium-centric concerns. I imagine the act of critical writing to be radical, one that can activate the political imagination. It helps us envision alternate readings and possibilities within a work. Unfortunately, criticality is often seen as an effort to diminish or "cancel" works, and not as a channel to foster debate.

What if criticality were built around the politics of care? For me, this would embody an accountability to our fellow citizens, not just those who are in the role of spectators and subjects, but also to our industry peers, as image-makers and thinkers. This "care" could be embodied in thinking about and building images, reflecting rigorously on how we see and what or whom we show, demanding more out of the practice and building a collective conscience towards questioning the conclusions we reach (or don't) with photographic narratives. In my practice, since I work mostly with images that are inevitably oriented towards the human experience and society, rather than form-based or conceptual experiments, these concerns have reverberations beyond our own industry.

This grounding in care could be a potent ingredient for criticality – in so much as we view it as collective learning, and as an instrument to dismantle the hierarchies that may emerge in the process. The critic, the image-author, the viewer as well as the practice itself stand to be enriched if we were to build systems that nurture criticality as well as the response to it. While there is no dearth of critical thinking, there are very few platforms that champion this kind of writing. Perhaps for criticality to thrive, it needs to exist outside of a capitalist structure, seen more through a discursive lens as an intellectual pursuit.

Perhaps this existing outside of capitalist structure brings us back to your desire to write for yourself? Have you found tactics for writing which allow you to construct a space where writing functions in its own or in your own time?

What I mean by existing outside of a capitalist structure is that knowledge production cannot be beholden to profit. However, it requires institutional support to sustain itself, functioning akin to the academy but allowing a more fluid exchange with those outside of it. Those that have resources could (should?) divert them to this end, investing in a return far greater than any financial gain.

What stops me from writing for myself is time. The kind of writing I currently pursue does not pay commensurate to the labour it involves. For most of us, we are already functioning outside of this realm of profit-making, and the desire to write stems from a need to respond and engage. If support was extended to foster deeper engagement and thought, it could help in wrestling time away from other pursuits, and to move away from the need to constantly "produce".

Before I embark on the process of writing for myself, I need to drown out the noise, and listen. To "take in" more than I "put out in the world". Reading is a necessary precursor and an integral part of this process. For years, I have felt, that as grateful as I am for the writing invitations, I am compelled to respond immediately. While this works a different muscle, writing for myself involves a longer, more sustained engagement with a theme, one that perhaps assimilates many of my influences and experiences.

So the answer to your question is no, I haven't managed to construct this space, but I am hopeful that it will emerge as my practice evolves, or when someone reading this is compelled to help create it!

Afterword
Duncan Wooldridge

(With, Around and Alongside: Reflections on Writing Photography)

Duncan Wooldridge is an artist, writer and curator. He is Course Director for MA Fine Art Photography at Camberwell College of Arts, University of the Arts London, and is the author of John Hilliard: Not Black and White *(Ridinghouse, 2014) and* To Be Determined: Photography and the Future *(SPBH Editions, 2021). A founder of the Global Photographies Network, his research examines experimental photographic process, and art and photography's interconnections.*

Writing is in many ways a stretching of the self and a seeking of connections. Its act runs the gamut of encounter, self-reflection, critical articulation and position taking, imagination, proposition or the speculative. There can be no singular writing, only practices and revisions demarcated by fields and genres, across commonly adopted codes of communication, styles, given forms and rules.

When we set out the approach for this book, we hoped that its format would place a delicate balance between our voices as interlocutors, the responses of our invited respondents and also the crossovers, alignments and diverging paths of writing across a rich range of contributors. This is not the conventional dialogic form of conversation we might all be used to, but we recognised in the questionnaire a non-linear, spatial and contextual space for discourse that was rich in its cross-referencing, echoes and continuities, as well as its disconnections and variations.

That was one of the pleasures of reading and participating in the preceding volume, *Curator Conversations*: we got to see how different respondents had tackled the very same questions, with consonances and dissonances laid bare. We proposed for this series a subtle modification. We decided upon bookended contributions with reflections on writing and what we had found. We also added to the process an extra layer, following up where it seemed useful or necessary to extend ideas and open new space: each conversation was a process that permitted a mix of the common and the customised. No interview is exactly the same, but we hope there are plenty of grounds for layered readings.

It would be a convenient conceit to say that all of these contributions involved an identical process. In a few instances, writers' responses were spoken and transcribed, whilst other contributors either amalgamated their follow-up questions into their original responses, or responded so fully that little follow-up seemed necessary. All of this demonstrates writing and language's complex and decisive relationship to speech, the dynamics of conversation in its expanded forms, and the daily pressures of maintaining a practice as a writer in a field that almost always necessitates some other form of employment. There are few lofty platforms from which writers escape the everyday in order to write at a great remove.

Conversations we held about the interviews also grew beyond what was sometimes set to be presented here: questions about format, processes and clarifications, events in our lives and subsequent meetings when we found ourselves in the same city are all part of a practice that can often be, and be represented as, solitary, when the act is always a moving beyond the self.

One of the most striking realisations to emerge from the series was the frequency with which our interviewed writers described coming to their practices from the making or showing of images, working with photographs as a practice before the writing on photography takes place: we all know that images generate texts – today's heavily contextualised, socially-engaged practices make text required reading – but it is easily forgotten that the desire to write often emerges from those who have built a layered interest in the phenomena of images, where writing exists as but one practice or form of expression. Writers are image-makers, even though, on occasion, it can be customary to write as if only occupying the position of the near-mythical observer.

David Levi Strauss and Taco Hidde Bakker describe how their studies in photography were formative, working with decisions that are made in making images and sharing knowledge and positions. Study is a space where writing is encouraged, firstly as a form of oblique self-examination (young photographers are encouraged to write to see and become critical of their interests and decisions through the works of others). It becomes, over time, a methodology for itself, an ongoing interest in how seeing happens beyond the singular position of the *I*: to describe writing as complementary would be to suggest a parallel path where image and text never meet. Joanna Zylinska notes that a practice of making photographs once ran alongside her academic and published work before they intersected as they do today, describing a convergence where many writers on photography are also makers. Daniel C. Blight describes the making of image covers, and the frustrations of the rituals of photography becoming language in a frustrated incantation. The pleasures and obstructions around making and using photography are amongst the prompts which give rise to a compulsion to write, and an adoption of strategies beyond pure description, or pure explanation, might be seen as emerging from the dialogue between image-making and its reflections, which seek neither pole. It is interesting that a writer such as Blight has himself begun to make images regularly as part of a practice where his writing seeks a slowing down.

Writing about photography is a consistent cause of concern. Can we write about images adequately if we do not move beyond the passivity of observation? What are the appropriate methodologies for an object, such as the image – which communicates through an entirely different register, that of language? One position adopted by writers today is to articulate a shift relative to the image where writing "about" images has become what is described as a writing "with" or "around" the photograph. Such a subtle gesture is constructive because we know images neither from a position that is fully outside (writing about – a place where the critic would be a dominant shaper of meaning), nor from a place entirely inside (writing through – a space, equally, where the maker becomes the authority, as though they had full determining control). We are incapable of describing images completely, and each reading brings something that must be contended with.

To write *with* a photograph is to attempt to describe a position of collaboration, empathy or alignment. Subtle shifts have significant underlying motives and resulting consequences: by writing with the image, do we recognise its agency, so as to commune with it? Or do we in fact collaborate with its makers, and therefore support or reinforce its proposed positions? What are the methods of such a writing with or around, and how do they clarify what a writing with entails? A politics of care that precedes but was foregrounded in the Covid-19 pandemic brings into view the ethics and politics of written texts. Max Houghton describes her interest to write with photographs as emerging from the curatorial traditions of custodial responsibility traced with a feminist lineage: "[It] is important to me to impart the same kind of care in my writing as the photographer did in the original images." Houghton describes a shared responsibility she articulates as extending to a photograph's subject matter, to its maker and also to its depicted subjects, the world it figures, displays or reveals. She states with honesty: "I don't tend to write about work that doesn't move me," something which is rarely expressed but commonly practiced. When we are *moved* to write, writing is always a writing with or against. Alignments are subtle micro-political practices.

Reading a photograph today requires a sensitivity and patience which runs counter to the hurry of the attention economy. Close reading reveals subtle perspectives obscured by the consumption of information. Christopher Pinney describes the everyday or "demotic" photograph as having a radical political potential, constructing and shaping the demos as it is seen and reproduced, whilst Simon Njami states that, as a writer, he seeks the motivations behind an image because each image is always not just a way of seeing, but a form of expanded self-portraiture. We must learn from images and not just discourse, Pinney argues, reminding us that images are intelligent and influential objects. Like the written text, images model a way of thinking, seeing and acting in the world. Even though we recognise an image's power, we somehow assume that criticism must lay in judgement, confirming or denying that which the image proposes. Consequently, writing *with* seems to run counter to our expectation that a text has critical teeth. Yet here we have some work to do: the subtle differences of the role of essayist and critic describe specific practices that are conflated, as critical decisions also precede the process of writing (the decision to write at all), whilst the approach of a text, as an essay, a work of criticism or review, describes and articulates a position in and around the image. Criticality is not simply inside writing – it is in its ecologies. If we accept texts without recognising the presence of what Njami calls motivation, we risk reinforcing a perception of writing as pure information, a fiction indeed. Some texts may describe a process of judgement, but many direct themselves not to the validity of what is written about but give readings of what should be discussed, emphasised or given weight, having already decided that the image is a carrier of meaning and value.

This process to produce criticism involves an intense relationship, extended beyond curiosity and beyond immediate impact, sustained and developed over time. Tina M. Campt describes two such procedures in her generous, expansive account of her practice, one she has used for writing about photographs, and another as she has begun to adopt to write about contemporary art and moving image. With photography, the relative stasis of the image permits both looking and looking away. A writing with the photograph is a durational process, but recurring attentiveness reveals for Campt a subtle vibration where an image moves beyond what it shows to enable long-lasting and sometimes divergent impressions, frequencies and vibrations which change across time. The subjective impressions of the writer are permitted. This is brought into generous contact with what the work shows and insists upon. Campt's writing with recent installations and video works develops from a physical sitting, an intensive *accompanying*, a being with and writing *alongside* the work as it takes place. For anyone who has observed or invigilated both still and moving image artworks might know, for much of the day such works often play to empty rooms. Campt's keeping company comes with a sense that the work has something to say, describing, in its transmissibility, a desire to connect. Sitting with makes apparent the agency of the image, recognising a force where resonances and motivations show themselves more clearly.

By contrast with the affective act of writing with, the process of writing around the photographic image proposes a diagrammatical model, a mapping of how an image moves and makes forms of contact and interconnection. Understanding emerges from a kind of encircling – values and meanings are drawn from how the image intersects with language and other images. David Campany describes how images play active roles in his texts and books, imagery contributing to writing and displacing the dialectic where the image is either explained through text, or illustrates that which is written. The power of the writer, perhaps elided in an affective reading of companionship, is not denied here, but described as the writer orbits around the image, made visible as language circles and at times finds itself bound by the pull of the photograph. Attraction and propulsion function together. Force comes into contact with force.

Active descriptions of how writing approaches the image add a layer of detail to the sometimes-concealed production of discourse. They describe positions of writing from the beginning of its process through to its realisation, along all of its challenges and obstacles. Taous R. Dahmani's reminder that the essay has its root in effort – "*essayer*" in French is "to try" – follows her account of the self-discipline of getting down to writing, to a disciplinary training, producing a PhD, that is conditioned by exams and the expectations and traditions of the academy which often reproduces Its own ways of seeing and thinking. Dahmani's interest in the shortened essay form is as an outside to the confines or constraints of the academic text, though she shows too that this comparative freedom has a politics that also needs to observed. Why do we focus on form? Critique is often levelled at criticism when it emphasises or discusses the *formal*. Forms shape the ethics and thus the politics of what is produced. Dahmani usefully places us on the threshold between two modes: an *academic* writing that figures its ethics on a systematic attempt to step away from subjectivity, and a poetic or affective essayism that encourages the expression of socially framed experience, describes alignments and points of departure. Writing *with* is clearly the signal of a movement to embrace or recognise elements of the latter.

Within recent writing, the intersectional practice of identifying our contexts and agencies has begun to be foregrounded. Tanvi Mishra reflects upon, and puts into practice, *positionality* when she describes her interest in the photographer's place and role within image-making, also foregrounding her own caste identity and power as a writer and editor. What we do with the power that we have – and those who have regular access to forms of creative expression or publishing all have forms of power – are part of the politics of writing and image-making. As Mishra acutely observes, we must begin to ask what we are producing, what it reveals and fails to make visible. A pressing concern that writing might draw our attention towards is, she reminds us, "photography's inability, or limited ability, to shift the gaze towards the perpetrator, the oppressor, the coloniser." We must become more accustomed to a more complex regime of image-making and writing, as existing strategies clearly do not serve the radical purposes which criticism can often claim for them.

From the critique of Martha Rosler until today, practices have very gradually begun to foreground gestures and strategies of image-making, collaborative research and the assemblage of complex forms of truth-building, to make visible a system of power that often actively resists representation. The invisibility of the image-maker, and the colonial gaze of early photographic records which maintained, until very recently, a near-complete disappearance of the photographing agent, is itself a form of power. Writing and photography meet in a renewed space of storytelling. The decentring of dominant perspectives requires both a stepping forward and a stepping out of the way. Here, positional practices and academia grapple with what has been described in contemporary philosophy as the social construction of facts, doing so from opposite directions, acknowledging subjectivity and attempting to mitigate it. What matters is the attempt and its ongoing critical re-evaluation: criticism, we might also be reminded, exists as a long trajectory of parsing what is unnecessary from what is significant: its origin is the Greek "*krinein*", meaning to separate or divide.

Joanna Zylinska's project to "explore the constitution of the human" notes that we "are mediating our relationships with others through images." What we share with each other today is facilitated but also challenged by technological capitalism's grip on our time, as gestures and actions of seeking-equivalence and a micropolitics beyond the *I* in our daily interactions form important strands of shared experience. Olga Smith, who draws our attention to national boundaries but also the limits of geographies and the threats of nationalism, suggests that we must attempt to locate a common understanding beyond that of nation whilst recognising difference. For, as Zylinska notes, citing the philosopher Amanda Lagerkvist, the stakes are high: photography is an "existential medium," intricately interwoven with processes of sustaining life and facilitating death. Smith, Zylinska and Bakker each state the impossibility of approaching photography today without negotiating its multiple roles in the climate emergency. Photography is more closely intertwined with the mineral, social and political structures of our everyday encounter than we are encouraged to admit. A tracing of the uses of images in our everyday culture quickly reveals how closely inscribed the technologies of images are to the extractive practices of rare minerals and the cultivation of energy, pollution and climate disaster.

As Zoé Samudzi powerfully notes, photography's proximity to violence and its continual use, presence and recurrence in our social fields contains within it a deeply troubling acceptance, even a continuation or permission for violent acts shows the need for criticism to attend to not only what is shown, but what is constructed or facilitated by representational fields and our ways of using images. Samudzi is rare in running directly counter to a still dominant belief that the act of drawing attention is sufficient as ethical practice, stating: "[An] affective overhaul is in order, particularly in our understanding of empathy as a collective political emotion. […] As abject violence must occur again and again, what does it mean to watch it again and again?" Traversing climate emergency, racial and economic violence, writing might, but only might, serve to propel photography to address, communicate and impact our ways of living in the world. To do so, argues Samudzi with great persuasion: "[Criticality] should offer reflections on how to assimilate the things we view and the feelings that arise upon viewing into our everyday lives – a move to begin engaging and resolving that sense of arrest and despairing engulfment that John Berger describes in "Photographs of Agony" (1972): Novelty is nice, but a deep engagement of the quotidian and the taken for granted, especially when the quotidian is [existential] violence, is even better."

My role as a white male Western writer and editor – and our publication in English – provides a series of horizons delineating whose voices are included in this volume. As editors, we recognise

that when commissioning interviews, our access to English is both
a privilege and a limitation, which we sought to begin to confront.
We have attempted to reckon with the threshold of conscious and
unconscious positions we occupy by continuously reflecting on the
balances of genders, geographies, languages, occupations and
politics. We spent time consulting what in academia we sometimes
call critical friends, and sought recommendations from international
professionals to widen our selection – to make choices, as much
as possible in a short volume – to bring us into contact with
writers we had not met or had not read before in depth. There are
great discoveries here, as a result of the generous reading lists
and impassioned and affectionate support for writing: Samudzi's
affection for Kimberly Juanita Brown's "Regarding the Pain of the
Other: Photography, Famine and the Transference of Affect" (2014)
is just one such example. In our selection, only the smallest tip of an
iceberg of work that is to be done in decolonising, internationalising
and recognising the interconnected practices of photography is
evident. Deborah Willis describes how, in her training in photographic
history, she "missed stories of black culture and diverse stories of
women and work," leading her to "notice gaps" which her writing
has rigorously set out to reveal and populate with careful detail.
International gaps, and cross-cultural tools must follow.

Writing quickly travels a long way from the politics of form to the
forms of politics. Our hope is that *Writer Conversations* illustrates the
crucial roles writing and photography play in setting the conditions for
the world that is to come. To write about images – to connect to them,
write with and write around them – and to recognise the stakes of the
ecologies of our image worlds, is not only to produce a record. It is to
set an agenda. A statement that has stayed throughout the project of
this book is Tina M. Campt's final response in her interview: "I don't
want to be exceptional. I want to share a world with others where we
have some sense of equivalence. I think that's a beautiful world, as
opposed to the one where there are some who are exceptional and
others who are not." Writing can give voice and share tools, bringing
closer a world that we want to inhabit.

Epilogue
Tim Clark

Tim Clark is Editor in Chief of 1000 Words and Artistic Director for Fotografia Europea in Reggio Emilia, Italy, together with Walter Guadagnini, Director of CAMERA, Torino, Italy, and photo historian and researcher at Archive of Modern Conflict, Luce Lebart. He is also serving as curatorial advisor for the Discovery section of Photo London 2022 and 2023. Clark teaches on BA (Hons) Photography at The Institute of Photography, Falmouth University.

'Like two lovers lying next to each other in bed who can never know the others' mind.' This was the beautiful analogy summoned by Nicholas Muelnner when asked about his self-identification as an artist "who operates at the intersection of photography and writing." Muelnner went on to explain that the differences between language and representation are irreconcilable; 'unbridgeable autonomies'. Yet words and images migrate, exchange and intercourse, shifting back and forth between the visible and the articulable, exhibition and interpretation, suggesting and disclosing. The alleged muteness of images and inadequacies of words present a challenge to attempts to construct and administer meaning around an artwork, but still we try to further this gesture, even if it is destined for impossibility. Within these power dynamics and indeterminate relations, we've come to understand the important roles of collaboration and dialogue (as opposed to imposing fixed borders) between the textual and visual. After all, words ultimately turn into images, and images back into words. In this sense, their relationship is more dialectal trope than binary opposition.

As an online contemporary photography magazine celebrating its 15th anniversary in 2023, *1000 Words* commissions exhibition and photobook reviews, essays and interviews in response to the visual culture of our present moment. Founded in 2008, the editorial commitment has always been to explore the possibilities for the photography whilst stimulating debate around current modes of practice, curation, discourses and theory internationally. *1000 Words* is recognised for exploring and inhabiting the space between words and images through its investigations into the complex and changing ways photography shapes our understanding of the world.

Consequently, the magazine has built a substantial archive of knowledge from culturally diverse worlds of photography and is used as a resource for artists, educators, researchers, historians, critics and curators working internationally. *1000 Words* supports and provides a platform for an esteemed roster of contributors, having showcased and published both established names as well as new writers and artists, many of whom have gone on to be published (or exhibited) widely. *Writer Conversations*, edited by Duncan Wooldridge and Lucy Soutter, continues these efforts. In the process, it offers a panoramic view onto the premises and practices of writing on photography that have given rise to an array of critical commentary and intellectual histories shaping the medium of photography today.

We would like to extend our deepest thanks to the contributing writers who generously gave their time and energy to reflect on writing in the midst of their own busy schedules. We are grateful to Tim Clark, the series editor, for entrusting us with this highly enjoyable assignment and providing constructive input along the way. Our warm appreciation to Alex Merola for his hard work, tireless engagement and attention to detail, and to Sarah Boris for producing a beautiful book and series.

We would also like to acknowledge the University of Westminster's School of Arts and the CCW Graduate School, University of the Arts London for supporting our research. Thanks also to George and Violet Barber, David Bate, Jean Brundrit, Iona Fergusson, Doro Globus, Vincent Hasselbach, Teemu Hupli, Svea Josephy, Ulrike Leyens, Elisa Medde, Mucsi Emese, Sarah Pickering, Rashi Rajguru, Anshika Varma and Stanley Wolukau-Wanambwa.

Editors Duncan Wooldridge
and Lucy Soutter
Series Editor Tim Clark
Copy Editor Alex Merola
Art Direction & Design Sarah Boris
Printed and bound in Great Britain
by Clays Ltd, Elcograf S.p.A

1000 Words
29 The Arthaus
205 Richmond Road
London
E8 3FF
United Kingdom

info@1000wordsmag.com
www.1000wordsmag.com

ISBN 978-1-3999-3649-1

First published by 1000 Words Photography Ltd, 2023

Distribution

Antenne Books
The Sunroom, Hackney Downs Studios
17 Armhurst Terrace
London
E8 2 BT
United Kingdom

bryony@antennebooks.com
www.antennebooks.com
+44 (0)203 582 8257

Writer Conversations is edited by Lucy Soutter (University of Westminster) and Duncan Wooldridge (Camberwell College of Arts, University of the Arts London), upon the invitation of Tim Clark (*1000 Words* and The Institute of Photography, Falmouth University). It sits alongside *Curator Conversations*, edited by Tim Clark, first published in 2021.